Andreas Foerster and Naoko Tamura

Kanji ABC

A Systematic Approach to Japanese Characters

CHARLES E. TUTTLE COMPANY
Rutland · Vermont : Tokyo · Japan

German language edition published in 1992
by Max Hueber, Ismaning

Published by the Charles E. Tuttle Company, Inc.
of Rutland, Vermont & Tokyo, Japan
with editorial offices at
2-6 Suido 1-chome, Bunkyo-ku, Tokyo 112

LCC Card No. 93-61452
ISBN 0-8048-1957-2

First edition, 1994
Second printing, 1994

Printed in Japan

Table of Contents

Preface v
Introduction vii
Part I: Graphemes 1
Part II: Kanji 33
Grapheme Index 212
Stroke Count Index 218
Reading Index 222

List of Tables:
1. Origin of the Graphemes 252
2. Hiragana and Katakana Charts 253
3. Graphemes 254

Preface

In *Kanji ABC* a new approach is offered for studying and memorizing kanji, the characters used in the Japanese language. The 1,945 *jōyō kanji* recommended by the Japanese government for everyday use are introduced. This official list of characters has shaped the language, and thus reflects about 99% of the kanji used in newspapers. Because no previous knowledge of spoken Japanese or grammar is required, both beginners and advanced students who would like to review kanji can use this book.

In order to become literate in a character-oriented language, the student must deal with a large number of written characters in addition to learning the spoken language. Memorizing them is a separate learning process, and this is the greatest difficulty with such languages. It is even possible to develop a "silent literacy" to some extent, i.e., to understand a written text without being able to speak the language. The goal of this book is to organize and simplify the task of memorizing kanji. In order to concentrate on this, *Kanji ABC* does not contain notes on grammar or usage of the spoken language but rather offers a pragmatic strategy for students who wish to acquire this important building-block of the Japanese language in the most efficient manner.

This book will help to establish a solid base for the mastery of kanji. However, it is still not an easy task and much effort is required to reach this goal. Being able to read and write Japanese, though, is the reward, and this is absolutely essential to a real command of the language. This is something to remember when overwhelmed by the task from time to time, a feeling which anyone who studies kanji has certainly experienced.

The authors are indebted to a large number of people who contributed to the development of this book. In particular we wish to express our gratitude to Yuriko Motoi, Markus Waltner, Christine Handel, and the Charles E. Tuttle Company and its editorial staff. Although the objective of this book is not an academic one, much inspiration was also gained from Stalph's scientific analysis of kanji in his book "Grundlagen einer Grammatik der Sinojapanischen Schrift." Furthermore the following books were helpful for the creation of our approach:

De Roo, Joseph, R. 2001 Kanji, 2nd edition, Tokyo, 1982.
Habein, Yaeko S., Mathias Gerald B. The Complete Guide to Everyday Kanji, Tokyo, 1991.
Hadamitzky, Wolfgang, and Mark Spahn. Kanji & Kana, Tokyo, 1981.
Heisig, James W. Remembering the Kanji, 2nd edition, Tokyo, 1985.
Henshall, Kenneth. A Guide to Remembering Japanese Characters, Tokyo, 1988.
Karlgreen, Bernhard. Analytic Dictionary of Chinese and Sino Chinese, New York, 1974.

Kurotani, Naoemi et al. A New Dictionary of Kanji Usage, Tokyo, 1982.

Osaka University of Foreign Studies. The First Step to Kanji, Part 1 and Part 2, Osaka, 1969 and 1971.

Pye, Michael. The Study of Kanji, Revised Edition, Tokyo, 1984.

Stalph, Juergen. Grundlagen einer Grammatik der Sinojapanischen Schrift, Wiesbaden, 1989.

Stalph, Juergen. Kanji Theorie und Kanji-Studien in Japan seit 1945, Bochum, 1985.

Books in Japanese:

安藤淑子　坪井佐奈枝　「非漢字系学習者に対する初級前期の漢字指導の一試案」
日本語教育　２６号　１９７５

石井勲　連想式漢字記憶術－石井式漢字はむずかしくない　朝日ソノラマ　１９７５

岡田進　これなら楽しくできる　漢字の教え方－量と水道方式の発想による
太郎次郎社　再版　１９７９

貝塚茂樹　他　角川漢和中辞典　角川書店　第１３４版　１９７３

加藤常賢　漢字の起源　角川書店　第１０版　１９７７

加藤常賢　山田勝美　著　字源辞典　角川書店　再版　１９８５

岸陽子　「漢字教育　漢字の教え方」　講座日本語教育　第３分冊
早稲田大学語学教育研究所　第２版　１９８６

国立国語研究所　現代新聞の漢字　秀英出版　１９７６

国立国語研究所　文字・表記の教育　日本語教育指導参考書１４　大蔵省印刷局　１９８８

小林一仁　漢字教育の基礎研究　明治図書　１９８１

小林一仁　漢字の系統的指導　明治図書　１９８４

柴田道広　長崎武昭　山岸嵩　ＮＨＫおもしろ漢字ミニ字典　第３版　リヨン社
１９８９

下村昇　漢字の本　１年生 － ６年生　偕成社　１９８９

進藤秀幸　山田勝美　著　漢字の語源　角川書店　１９７７

武部良昭　漢字の教え方　アルク　１９８９

籐堂明保　漢字語源辞典　学燈社　１９６５

籐堂明保　漢字なりたち辞典　第１０版　教育社　１９９０

藤原宏　新版漢字書き順字典　第一法規　１９９０

藤原宏　注解　常用漢字表　ぎょうせい　１９８１

真武直　漢字形音義の構造論的体系研究　日本学術振興会　１９７６

村上久吉　字原を探る　業文社　１９７８

諸橋轍次　他　新漢和辞典　大修館書店　第３版　１９８５

山田勝美　生きていた絵文字の世界　玉川大学出版部　１９７７

Introduction

The Japanese Language

In written Japanese three sets of characters are used in addition to roman letters *(romaji)*, which are only used to abbreviate or highlight words. These sets of characters are kanji and the two syllabaries *hiragana* and *katakana*. As shown on page 253, both of the syllabaries are phonetic alphabets consisting of 46 syllables developed from simplified Chinese characters. *Hiragana* are used for Japanese words that cannot be expressed in kanji or have grammatical functions, while the use of *katakana* is mainly restricted to foreign names or expressions adapted to Japanese so that they can be expressed with the syllables available.

There is a good reason for continued use of all three character sets, although any Japanese word can be written phonetically with one of the two syllabaries. Many words are pronounced alike (homophones), so kanji are required in order to avoid ambiguity in the written language. Therefore, is not likely that kanji will become obsolete in the near future. Both syllabaries and kanji can be transliterated into *romaji* with 22 roman letters. In this book the Hepburn system of romanization, which is most widely accepted, is used.

Kanji

When Chinese characters for words and expressions were introduced in Japan toward the end of the fourth century, they had a strong impact on the Japanese language. As a result, many kanji have two pronunciations: the *kun* reading is the Japanese pronunciation, and the *on* reading is the Chinese pronunciation that has been adjusted to Japanese sounds. The fact that there are no different vocal pitches (tones) in spoken Japanese is the main reason for the many homophones.

Kanji were not introduced to all parts of Japan at the same time or in the same form. Therefore several *on* readings may exist for one kanji, although some of these *on* readings are rarely used in modern Japanese. The *on* readings presented in this book were selected on the basis of a study of frequency of occurrence conducted by the National Institute for Japanese Language (*Kokuritsu kokugo kenkyūjo*), thus less-frequently used *on* readings are not presented.

The *on* readings are used mainly in pronouncing combinations of two or more kanji (compounds). In the third column in Part II of this book, they are written in capital letters. If a kanji is used as an individual character, the Japanese or *kun* reading is generally used. This reading is given in small letters.

The Problem of Memorizing Kanji

Japanese children study kanji for at least nine years in school. Even so, people in Japan often find they need to refer to a kanji dictionary when reading or writing. How can foreign students, who are usually older, have little time, and are rarely confronted with such characters in everyday life manage this task? Due to the perceived impossibility of the task, the study of kanji is excluded from the start in the curricula of many Japanese courses.

A particular problem is that Western students are accustomed to a phonetically oriented writing system, i.e. one in which the letters of the alphabet are linked to a specific pronunciation. As shown above, a kanji can have two or more readings and there are many homophones. Therefore the association of a kanji with its pronunciation is problematic. To learn a kanji by memorizing the order of strokes in which it is written is also difficult. The student has to cope with abstract graphical structures unrelated to his or her previous knowledge of writing symbols. As a consequence, the student's visual memory may prove to be less powerful than expected, and this explains a large part of the problem with memorizing kanji.

Solving the Kanji Problem

Kanji ABC shows that the key to a successful study of kanji lies in breaking down the complex characters into familiar ones. To accomplish this, the approach must be different from those methods based on writing kanji repeatedly, which is an appropriate method for Japanese children. The idea behind *Kanji ABC* is to reveal the structure and the pictures that make up the kanji. This is based on the didactic rule that a well-structured context is much easier to memorize than a bundle of unrelated facts. When new information can be related to information that is already known, it becomes easier to remember. Of course, every student can devise his or her own structure after several years of studying kanji, but this takes time, and even so is not guaranteed to be successful.

Therefore the sequence in which kanji are introduced is crucial. When graphically simple kanji are introduced first, they can be used as components for more complicated kanji. This is not possible when the sequence of introduction is determined by the importance of a kanji. In many cases, graphically simple forms are rarely used and would therefore be introduced only after the more complex but more frequently used kanji.

While it takes at least two years to become familiar with the most important kanji using the traditional method, this approach enables the student to accomplish this in a much shorter time. It is no longer necessary to use the importance of a kanji to determine when it should be introduced; learning kanji in a didactic sequence is quicker and retention is greater.

Dividing Complex Kanji into Graphemes

In order to master a kanji, it is important to divide it into smaller elements. As early as the second century, Chinese characters were classified into 540 groups, principally so they could be arranged in a lexicographical order and located in a dictionary.

In eighteenth-century China this classification was standardized into the 214 "historical radicals." During the course of adaptation in Japan some dictionaries incorporated more, others less than 214 radicals. Since the main purpose was to locate kanji in dictionaries, not all of the kanji elements are covered by the radicals. Some parts of a kanji remain undefined and are described as "residual stroke-count," making it impossible to compose a kanji from its elements.

Kanji ABC divides kanji not for lexicographical but for didactic reasons, and covers all the elements of kanji. These elements are termed graphemes. For the most part they are comprised of basic kanji and historical radicals. About a third of the graphemes are neither basic kanji nor radicals, but frequent combinations of other graphemes used to avoid unreasonable fragmentation of kanji. Table 1 presents an overview of the graphemes according to their origin.

All *jōyō kanji* can be constructed by combining these graphemes, and elongated or contracted forms are still interpreted as the same graphemes. Using this definition of graphemes, more than 70% of all *jōyō kanji* can be constructed with two or less graphemes. More than 90% consist of one to three graphemes. Graphemes can also be used as a basis for constructing kanji not included in the list of *jōyō kanji.* Since the graphemes include all historical radicals, except for a few which are no longer used, the adaptation to any radical system will not be a problem.

Naming the Graphemes

All the graphemes are linked to expressions in everyday life. Since abstract stroke orders are now replaced by familiar terms, hitherto unused parts of the brain can be activated. A quick glance at Part II of the book shows that the meaning of a kanji is often related to the meaning of its graphemes. This is not accidental; on the contrary, the graphemes were named according to their etymology. It is possible to imagine how many kanji were developed, and this helps the student memorize them.

Graphemes, however, also include graphical forms that became identical as the characters evolved. In addition, the etymological interpretations are often ambiguous. For teaching purposes it is not useful to confront the student with all of the different meanings of graphemes. Therefore, compromises were made in the naming of some graphemes, for which we must beg forgiveness.

These etymologically-based graphemes are powerful memory aids. Abstract stroke combinations suddenly become combinations of terms familiar to the student. A feeling for each kanji can be created. This method is similar to the natural process of remembering: new information is linked to existing impressions and feelings.

Kanji Compounds (Jukugo)

This book does not deal with kanji compounds, since combining a study system for kanji and a dictionary for compounds would lead to a compromise in quality and neither purpose would be served. Since individual interests vary, the presentation of a limited number of compounds may not fit to the vocabulary required by different students. It is more practical to study kanji compounds when they occur in the context of study material used for learning Japanese. There are special extensive dictionaries for compounds; the three most important are cross-referenced in the sixth column in Part II of this book.

It is most economical to focus on compounds after having studied the meanings of their single-kanji components. One problem with this method is that several kanji have somewhat divergent meanings. In response, this book concentrates on teaching the core meaning of the kanji, which will open the door to understanding and then memorization of compounds.

Knowing the core meaning of a kanji enables the student to link new compounds to previously learned kanji. A complete picture of Japanese writing will develop in logical progression: graphemes-kanji-compounds. Because of this, *Kanji ABC* may be used along with any other material for learning Japanese. Although all required graphemes and kanji are introduced, kanji compounds not needed in the learning material or in everyday use will not clutter the memory.

Organization of This Book

Kanji ABC is divided into two sections. In Part I, the graphemes are introduced step-by-step. Similar graphemes are classified into 26 groups, as shown in the table on pages 254 and 255. Each group is marked with a letter of the alphabet, in order to categorize it within a familiar structure.

In Part II, kanji that can be created from the graphemes already introduced plus a new grapheme are presented. With this sequence one can gradually become familiar with kanji. Similar kanji are introduced next to each other, reducing the danger of confusing them since the differences become obvious in close comparison. At first glance, the characters introduced on any page of Part II may seem very similar; however, after studying the differences carefully, the student is less likely to confuse them. Furthermore, since new kanji often consist of combinations of previously introduced kanji, studying a new one will reinforce that which has already been learned.

As the learning progresses, it will become apparent that many graphemes determine the *on* reading of a kanji. In the sequence of this book, kanji with the same *on* reading are often presented right next to each other, allowing the student to memorize them more easily. For example, all six kanji in group Y 10 have the same *on* reading, "HŌ." In other cases, however, the groups are not homogeneous, so it may be helpful to highlight readings that are the same.

Using This Book

Kanji ABC is especially well-suited to individual study because it allows the student to pace himself. Studying in a group may be useful as well because it is livelier and may increase effectiveness. There are two possible ways to use this book. The student will benefit most if his or her knowledge of graphemes and kanji increases step-by-step. Therefore, after having learned the basic graphemes, Grapheme Group A in Part I should be studied first, and then the corresponding kanji of Group A in Part II. With this alternating system between Part I and Part II for each group, the close relationship between graphemes and kanji can be appreciated. Even full-time students should not study more than one group per day, however.

Due to time limitations, such concentrated learning may not always be possible. Here, an inductive approach to study lends itself to benefit from the system of this book. First, all meanings of the graphemes in Part I should be learned as a foundation. Then, new kanji should be located in *Kanji ABC* as they come up. By studying the construction of a kanji, all graphemes will be reviewed systematically. It is also helpful to note the differences between the kanji that was looked up and the kanji immediately before and after it to decrease the possibility of confusing them later.

Whichever strategy is chosen, review will be necessary. It is useful to review the graphemes in Part I first and then the kanji in Part II. Since the information is in columns, the part to be reviewed can be covered with a sheet of paper.

The Graphemes in Part I

The graphemes in Part I are classified into groups for easier learning. First, the basic graphemes used most often are introduced according to their characteristic position within a kanji: LE=left, RI=right, TO=top, BO=bottom, EN=enclosure, FR=free. These graphemes are only used as a base; no kanji in Part II are directly related to them.

The remaining graphemes are separated into 26 groups of graphically similar forms, each designated by a letter of the alphabet. The groups A and Z are exceptions because the graphemes in them have no similarity. For groups B through Y, the second row from the top of the table on the back-cover page shows the common characteristics of the group.

The small numbers surrounding the graphemes in Part I refer to stroke order. As a general rule, the stroke order goes from top to bottom and from left to right. Lines are counted as one stroke even if they are curved. When the same stroke order is used in different graphemes, the number in brackets refers to the grapheme in which it appeared first. With this system, confusion with other, similar stroke orders is reduced, and graphemes with the same stroke orders may be repeated.

Finally, a meaning is assigned to each grapheme. The same word is used for different graphical forms, with only four exceptions: man (LE 5 and A 3), hand (LE 11 and G 8), small (TO 2 and A 12), and water (LE 2 and P 1). For LE 24, RI 8, BO 5, LE 8, and RI 3 a different expression was used despite the same graphical form to indicate a different position within the kanji.

The Kanji in Part II

In the **first column** the number of the grapheme group is given, and this refers to the number used in Part I. The kanji in the **second column** is printed in *minchō-tai* type, the most common type in Japan. Its vertical lines are relatively bold, and the horizontal strokes are finer. If a kanji is written in this way by hand, however, it resembles the handwriting of a primary school student. For everyday use, a semi-cursive style (*gyōsho*) or cursive style (*sōsho*) is used to allow more rapid writing.

If one wants to restrict oneself to writing with a word processor (*wapuro*) or a personal computer, it is not necessary to practice the handwritten forms. Still, in order to become familiar with the character, writing it at least once is recommended. For typing, roman letters are used as given in the **third column**. As mentioned before, the *kun* reading is written in small letters and the *on* reading in capital letters.

The core meaning of the kanji is given in the **fourth column**. Whenever the *on* reading is a nominalization of the *kun* reading, the meaning of the noun is not explicitly given. When a kanji can be used as a component of another kanji, but is not a grapheme in Part I, its meaning is printed in italics. Some Japanese verbs exist in *tadōshi* and *jidōshi* pairs which roughly correspond to English "transitive" and "intransitive" verbs. *Tadōshi* literally means other-moving word, while *jidōshi* means self-moving word. Although they have the same verbal base, the ending indicates to which of the two forms they belong. In the English meaning this difference is marked by (vt) or (vi).

In the **fifth column** the meanings of the graphemes are listed in the sequence in which they are written. If there is a slight variation in form, the grapheme is given in brackets. If a kanji is used as a component, its meaning is given. All graphemes and kanji used as components for more complex kanji are listed alphabetically in the grapheme index.

The **sixth column** provides cross-references to the following three dictionaries for kanji compounds:

1. Spahn, Mark and Hadamitzky, Wolfgang. Japanese Character Dictionary, 1989
2. Halpern, Jack. New Japanese-English Character Dictionary, 1990
3. Nelson, Andrew. The Modern Reader's Japanese English Character Dictionary, 1974

The following indexes have been included for locating unknown kanji and graphemes:

- Grapheme index
- Stroke count index
- Reading index

Depending on how intensively the book is studied, the grapheme group table may also be used to find unknown kanji. A kanji can be located under the grapheme that is introduced last of all the kanji's components. It should be remembered, however, that this separation was not devised for lexicographical reasons, but rather for didactic purposes.

Part I: Graphemes

Grapheme Group Left

冫	1 ice	犭	10 watchdog	酉	19 wine
氵	2 water	扌	11 hand	飠	20 eat
忄	3 feeling	礻	12 altar (of the ancestors)	金	21 metal
丬	4 bed	衤	13 robe	馬	22 horse
亻	5 human being	糸	14 thread	日	23 sun
禾	6 rice seedling	王	15 king	月	24 part of the body
米	7 rice	木	16 tree, wood		
阝	8 fortress	言	17 words		
弓	9 bow	⻊	18 foot		

Grapheme Group Right - Top

彡	1 style	䒑	1 horns	⺍	9 gather
刂	2 sword	⺌	2 small	爫	10 caress
阝	3 city wall	マ	3 typical	𠂉	11 human
卩	4 seal	⺈	4 tied up	⻗	12 rain
攵	5 teacher	宀	5 house		
頁	6 head	⺾	6 flower		
隹	7 chicken	⺮	7 bamboo		
月	8 moon	罒	8 net		

Grapheme Group Enclosure - Bottom - Free

厂	1 cliff	八	1 animal legs	丶	1 drop
广	2 building	儿	2 legs	氺	2 very much
疒	3 sickness	心	3 heart	丨	3 halve
辶	4 traveler	灬	4 cooking fire	卜	4 divining rod
夂	5 big step	月	5 part of the body	巾	5 cloth
囗 (last)	6 enclosed			土	6 earth
				大	7 big

Grapheme Group A

一	1 one	刀	10 sword	凵	19 container
二	2 two	女	11 woman	斤	20 ax
人	3 human being	小	12 small	丘	21 hill
山	4 mountain	少	13 little	羽	22 feather
石	5 stone	皿	14 plate		
耳	6 ear	子	15 child		
火	7 fire	母	16 mother		
川	8 river	父	17 father		
力	9 power	乂	18 scissors		

Grapheme Group B

口	1 mouth	𠂤	10 officer				
言	2 words (LI17)	呂	11 management (B1, FR1, B1)				
占	3 divine (FR4,B1)	中	12 middle				
加	4 add (A9, B1)	虫	13 insect (B12, ...)				
召	5 summon (honorific) (A10,B1)	中	14 middle course (B12, A1)				
豆	6 bean (A1, B1, OB1)	串	15 central point (B1, B1, FR3)				
兄	7 older brother (B1, UN2)						
兑	8 satan (..., B7)						
自	9 chief						

Grapheme Group C

日	1 sun, day	良	10 good (FR1, C9)	貝	19 money (shell) (C13, UN1)
旦	2 sunrise (C1, A1)	鳥	11 bird	則	20 rule (C19, RE2)
亘	3 period of time (A1, C1, A1)	車	12 vehicle (C3, FR3)		
旧	4 former (FR3, A1)	目	13 eye		
白	5 white (FR1, A1)	相	14 mutual (LI16, C13)		
原	6 original (BG1, C5, A12)	且	15 additionally		
百	7 hundred (A1, C5)	自	16 nose (self) (FR1, C13)		
門	8 gate	首	17 neck (OB1, C16)		
艮	9 solid	見	18 see (C13, UN2)		

Grapheme Group D

田	1 rice field	甲	10 first in a series (C1, FR3)		
苗	2 seedling (OB6, D1)	申	11 report (C1, FR3)		
畐	3 prosperity (A1, B1, D1)	里	12 countryside (D10, A2)		
魚	4 fish (OB4, D1, UN4)	単	13 single (OB9, C1, A1, FR3)		
曽	5 augment (..., D1, C1)	果	14 fruit (C1, ...)		
由	6 reason				
亩	7 alms (A1, C1, FR3)				
曲	8 bend				
曹	9 comrade (A1, D8, C1)				

Grapheme Group E

丁	1 block of houses	寸	10 a bit of		
了	2 finish	付	11 attach (LI5, E10)		
矛	3 halberd (OB3, ...)	寺	12 Buddhist temple (FR6, E10)		
可	4 possibility (E1, B1)	専	13 exclusive (D7, E10)		
奇	5 unusual (FR7, E4)				
牙	6 tusk				
示	7 show (A2, A12)				
于	8 expanse				
才	9 talent				

Grapheme Group F

十	1 ten	羊	10 sheep (OB1, A2, FR3)		
斗	2 bucket (..., F1)	半	11 half (OB1, A1, FR3)		
古	3 old (F1, B1)	丰	12 barrier		
固	4 hard (BG6, F3)	韋	13 thief (..., B1, F12)		
早	5 early (C1, F1)				
卓	6 fog (F1, C1, F1)				
干	7 dry (A2, FR3)				
缶	8 vibrate (OB10, F7, A19)				
平	9 flat				

Grapheme Group G

千	1 thousand	垂	10 hang down		
舌	2 tongue (G1, B1)	彳	11 step		
重	3 heavy (..., C1, ...)	行	12 go (G11, A1, E1)		
禾	4 rice seedling (LI6)	升	13 bottle		
釆	5 number	隹	14 chicken (RE7)		
壬	6 porter				
廷	7 court (G6, BG5)				
手	8 hand				
乗	9 ride				

Grapheme Group H

牛	1 cattle	乍	10 generate		
告	2 notify (..., B1)	竹	11 bamboo (OB7)		
先	3 earlier (..., UN2)				
生	4 life				
朱	5 vermilion				
失	6 lose				
矢	7 arrow				
午	8 noon				
隺	9 eagle (OB11, A1, G14)				

Grapheme Group I

士	1 scholar	並	10 line up	⺷	19 lamb's wool (..., I17)
吉	2 good luck (I1, B1)	亜	11 Asia		
土	3 earth (FR6)	西	12 west		
赤	4 red (I3, ...)	龶	13 cultivate		
圭	5 heap of earth (I3, I3)	菫	14 inferior (OB6, B1, ...)		
孝	6 filial piety (I3, ..., A15)	青	15 blue (I13, UN5)		
者	7 working person (I3, ..., C1)	責	16 responsibility (I13, C19)		
工	8 handicraft	王	17 king (LI15)		
五	9 five	主	18 master (FR1, I17)		

Grapheme Group J

木	1 tree, wood	米	10 rice (LI7)		
采	2 harvest (OB10, J1)	束	11 bundle (..., B1, ...)		
喿	3 bird's nest (B1, B1, B1, J1)	東	12 east (..., C1, ...)		
林	4 forest (J1, J1)				
麻	5 hemp (BG2, J4)				
本	6 basis (J1, A1)				
未	7 not yet (A1, J1)				
末	8 last part (A1, J1)				
朮	9 resin (J1, FR1)				

Grapheme Group K

冄	1 nosegay (F1, ...)	龷	10 herbs		
开	2 with both hands	昔	11 former times (K10, C1)		
廾	3 flexible	共	12 joint (K10, UN1)		
廿	4 leather				
革	5 reform (K4, B1, F1)				
甘	6 sweet				
某	7 a certain (K6, J1)				
其	8 game (..., UN1)				
井	9 well				

Grapheme Group L

冖	1 cover	咼	10 danger (..., L6, B1)	冊	19 counter for books (L6, ...)
𭕄	2 school house (OB9, L1)	岡	11 steel (L6, OB1, A4)	再	20 again (A1, L6, ...)
尚	3 elite (OB2, L1, B1)	而	12 beard	冓	21 structure (..., L20)
売	4 sell (I1, L1, UN2)	禺	13 scorpion (C1, L6, ...)	舟	22 ship
軍	5 army (L1, C12)	月	14 moon, month (LI24)	几	23 table
冂	6 cavity	肖	15 resemble (OB2, L14)	凡	24 common (L23, FR1)
内	7 inside (L6, A3)	用	16 use (L14, FR3)		
同	8 same (L6, A1, B1)	甫	17 fishing rod (A1, L14, FR3, FR1)		
周	9 periphery (L6, FR6, B1)	円	18 circle		

Grapheme Group M

亠	1 cap	亦	10 pink (see I4)	[illegible]	19 counsel
[illegible]	2 watchtower (M1, B1)	立	11 stand	[illegible]	20 stamina (M11, ...)
京	3 capital (M2, A12)	咅	12 group of people (M11, B1)		
市	4 market (M1, FR5)	音	13 sound (M11, C1)		
亡	5 deceased	章	14 chapter (M13, F1)		
方	6 direction	意	15 will (M13, UN3)		
文	7 writings	亲	16 first time (M11, J1)		
斉	8 equal (M7, ...)	辛	17 hot (M11, F1)		
交	9 intermingle (M1, A17)	[illegible]	18 emperor		

Grapheme Group N

乚	1 hook	化	10 change into (LI5, N9)	电	19 lightning (C1, N1)
乙	2 second class	比	11 compare (..., N9)	九	20 nine
心	3 heart	北	12 north (..., N9)	卆	21 angle of 90° (N20, F1)
必	4 without fail	旨	13 purport (N9, C1)	丸	22 round (N20, FR1)
穴	5 airhole (OB5, UN2)	兆	14 trillion	㔾	23 characteristic
元	6 origin (A2, UN2)	七	15 seven	巴	24 snake
酉	7 wine (LI19)	虍	16 tiger (FR4, ..., N15)	也	25 wriggle
尢	8 sink	毛	17 hair		
匕	9 crouch	屯	18 barracks		

Grapheme Group O

止	1 stop	是	10 fair (C1, O6)		
歩	2 walk (O1, A13)				
延	3 extend (..., O1, BG5)				
卸	4 wholesale (OB11, A1, O1, RE4)				
正	5 correct (A1, O1)				
疋	6 constant				
疋	7 dance (O6)				
足	8 suffice (B1, O6)				
走	9 run (FR6, O6)				

Grapheme Group P

水	1 water	辰	10 tremble (BG1, A1, P8)		
永	2 eternal	氏	11 family		
求	3 seek	氐	12 low (P11, A1)		
	4 far	民	13 people		
	5 grief	以	14 increase		
襄	6 complicated (M1, UN1, ..., P5)	卯	15 outside (..., A10)		
衣	7 clothes (M1, P5)	卬	16 protector (..., RE4)		
	8 mourning				
長	9 long (..., P8)				

Grapheme Group Q

厶	1 oneself	充	10 fill (Q8, UN2)		
台	2 platform (Q1, B1)	鬼	11 devil (FR1, D1, UN2, Q1)		
能	3 ability (Q1, L14, N9, N9)	亥	12 kernel (M1, ...)		
広	4 wide (BG2, Q1)	幺	13 fiber		
云	5 cloud (A2, Q1)	𢆶	14 strengthen (Q13, Q13)		
至	6 arrive (A1, Q1, FR6)	玄	15 profound (M1, Q13)		
去	7 go away (FR6, Q1)	糸	16 thread (LI14)		
𠫓	8 development (M1, Q1)	系	17 lineage (..., Q16)		
育	9 raise (Q8, UN5)				

Grapheme Group R

又	1 moreover	支	10 branch (F1, R1)		
取	2 take (A6, R1)	皮	11 skin (..., R1)		
叔	3 uncle (FR4, A1, A12, R1)				
隻	4 one of a pair (G14, R1)				
祭	5 festival (L14, R1, E7)				
殳	6 strike (L23, R1)				
圣	7 vertical (R1, FR6)				
奴	8 slave (A11, R1)				
反	9 against (BG1, R1)				

Grapheme Group S

奂	1 trade (OB4, ..., UN2, FR7)	昜	10 heat (C1, A1, S8)	名	19 name (S17, B1)
免	2 escape from (OB4, ..., UN2)	豕	11 pork belly	歹	20 death (A1, S17)
勹	3 envelope	家	12 home (OB5, S11)	列	21 row (S20, RE2)
勺	4 scoop (S3, FR1)	㒸	13 boar (..., S11)	久	22 long duration
句	5 phrase (S3, B1)	豤	14 intimate (..., C9)	夂	23 march
旬	6 ten-day period (S3, C1)	欠	15 lack	复	24 fold (OB11, C1, S23)
曷	7 dry up (C1, S3, N9)	次	16 next (LI1, S15)	发	25 stimulate (Q1, UN2, S23)
勿	8 never (S3, ...)	夕	17 evening	各	26 each (S23, B1)
万	9 ten thousand	舛	18 opposition (S17, F12)		

Grapheme Group T

	1 volcano	合	10 fit (T2, A1, B1)		
𠆢	2 roof	㑒	11 check (T2, A1, B1, A3)		
介	3 be in between (T2, ...)	俞	12 conversion (T2, A1, L14, RE2)		
余	4 leave over (T2, A2, A12)	侖	13 logic (T2, A1, L19)		
金	5 metal (LI21)	八	14 eight		
舎	6 barn (T2, FR6, B1)	公	15 public (T14, Q1)		
食	7 eat (T2, C10)	㕣	16 run out (T14, B1)		
命	8 command (T2, A1, ...)	谷	17 valley (..., T2, B1)		
今	9 now (T2, A1, ...)	丌	18 stool (A1, UN1)		

Grapheme Group U

尸	1 behind				
辟	2 prison (U1, B1, M17)				
尺	3 measure (U1, ...)				
戸	4 door (A1, U1)				
扁	5 enlarge (U4, L19)				
倉	6 storehouse (T2, A1, ..., B1)				

Grapheme Group V

右	1 right (..., B1)	莫	10 concealed (OB6, C1, V9)	夾	19 pinch
有	2 have (..., L14)	犬	11 dog (V9, FR1)	龹	20 document
布	3 linen (..., FR5)	賚	12 recover (V9, ..., C1, A12)	𡗗	21 fact
[illegible]	4 reality	天	13 heaven (A1, V9)	丰	22 long life
𠂇	5 stable	关	14 from heaven (OB1, V9)		
友	6 friend (V5, R1)	夫	15 husband (A1, V9)		
史	7 history (B1, ...)	𦰩	16 difficult (OB6, B1, V15)		
更	8 grow late (A1, C1, ...)	夬	17 choice		
大	9 big (FR7)	央	18 center		

Grapheme Group W

弋	1 ritual	戌	10 rear cover		
弍	2 lance (..., W1)	成	11 become		
代	3 substitute (LI5, W1)	戋	12 superficial		
戈	4 weapon				
𢦏	5 injure (F1, W4)				
戠	6 weaving loom (M13, ...)				
我	7 one's own				
義	8 righteousness (I19, W7)				
戊	9 grow				

Grapheme Group X

彐	1 broom	君	10 you (..., B1)		
翟	2 interval (X1, X1, G14)	争	11 contend (OB4, ...)		
𠬶	3 douse (X1, L1, R1)				
帚	4 cleanse (X1, L1, FR5)				
录	5 copper (X1, ..., FR2)				
肀	6 broomstick				
隶	7 sin (X6, FR2)				
聿	8 paintbrush				
兼	9 concurrently (OB1, ..., ...)				

Grapheme Group Y

匚	1 box	包	10 wrap (S3, Y9)		
区	2 division (..., A18, ...)	弓	11 bow (LI9)		
匹	3 comparable (..., UN2, ...)	弔	12 condolence (Y11, FR3)		
巨	4 huge	弗	13 cook up (Y11, ...)		
臣	5 minister	丂	14 dirty		
𦣝	6 oversee (Y5, OB11, A1)	考	15 think		
臤	7 massive (Y5, R1)	与	16 give (..., A1)		
馬	8 horse (LI22)	呉	17 kingdom of Wu (China) (B1, ..., T18)		
己	9 ego				

Grapheme Group Z

乚	1 corner	亅	10 take care	敝	19 bank note (OB2, L6, A12, RE5)
𠂤	2 rank	之	11 too little	鬲	20 ditch (A1, B1, L6,UN2,...)
非	3 negative assessment	為	12 do for the sake of	世	21 the world
不	4 negation of condition	入	13 enter	亟	22 troubled (A1, FR1, C13, ...)
無	5 negation of existence	屰	14 face to face (OB1, A19, ...)		
片	6 one-sided	敢	15 brave (..., A6, RE5)		
厂	7 circulation	身	16 body		
乃	8 spectacular	产	17 pretty (BG6, ...)		
及	9 reach to	刂	18 long sword		

Part II: Kanji

A1	一	hito(tsu), ICHI	one	grapheme	0a1.1, 3341, 1
A1	上	a(garu/geru), nobo(ru), ue, JŌ	raise, *rise*, up	divining rod, one	2m1.1, 3404, 798
A1	下	sa(garu/geru), shita kuda(saru), GE,KA	*lower*, down, give to an inferior	one, divining rod	2m1.2, 3378, 9
A1	光	hika(ru), hikari, KŌ	shine, *light*	small, one, legs	3n3.2, 2391, 1358
A2	二	futa, futa(tsu), NI	two	grapheme	0a2.1, 1922, 273
A2	仁	JIN	virtue, benevolence	human being, two	2a2.8, 20, 349
A2	三	mi, mit(tsu), SAN	*three*	one, two	0a3.1, 1924, 8
A3	人	hito, NIN, JIN	human being	grapheme	2a0.1, 3368, 339
A3	囚	SHŪ	prisoner	enclosed, human being	3s2.1, 3042, 1024
A3	座	suwa(ru), ZA	sit, seat	building, human being, human being, earth	3q7.2, 3116, 1515
A4	山	yama, SAN	mountain	grapheme	3o0.1, 2940, 1407

A4	仙	SEN	*hermit*	human being, mountain	2a3.1, 32, 359
A4	峠	tōge	mountain pass	mountain, rise, lower	3o6.3, 358, 1416
A4	出	de(ru), da(su), SHUTSU	*go out*, put out (stroke order!)	(mountain), (mountain)	0a5.22, 3498, 97
A4	拙	SETSU	clumsy, unskillful	hand, go out	3c5.11, 315, 1880
A5	石	ishi, SEKI	stone	grapheme	5a0.1, 2971, 3176
A5	拓	TAKU	break up farmland	hand, stone	3c5.1, 317, 1873
A5	岩	iwa, GAN	rock	mountain, stone	3o5.10, 2235, 1414
A6	耳	mimi, JI	ear	grapheme	6e0.1, 3516, 3697
A6	恥	haji(ru), haji, ha(zukashii), CHI	feel ashamed, shame, shy	ear, heart	6e4.2, 1313, 3704
A6	摂	SETSU	act in place of	hand, ear, very much	3c10.5, 650, 1976
A7	火	hi, KA	fire	grapheme	4d0.1, 3463, 2743

A7	灰	hai, KAI	*ash*	cliff, fire	2p4.1, 2979, 820
A7	炭	sumi, TAN	coal	mountain, ash	3o6.5, 2257, 1418
A7	煩	wazura(u/wasu), HAN	worry about (vi), trouble (vt)	fire, head	4d9.1, 1022, 2782
A7	秋	aki, SHŪ	*autumn*	rice seedling, fire	5d4.1, 1139, 3273
A7	愁	ure(i), SHŪ	sad, melancholy	autumn, heart	4k9.16, 2829, 1729
A7	炎	hoṇō, EN	*flame*, inflammation	fire, fire	4d4.4, 2420, 2751
A7	淡	awa(i), TAN	light-colored, faint	water, flame	3a8.15, 528, 2602
A7	談	DAN	conversation	words, flame	7a8.7, 1569, 4388
A8	川	kawa, SEN	river	grapheme	0a3.2, 6, 1447
A8	訓	KUN	instruction	words, river	7a3.6, 1454, 4317
A8	順	JUN	order, sequence	river, head	9a3.2, 18, 1450

A8	巡	megu(ru), JUN	go around, patrol	river, traveler	2q3.3, 3047, 4667
A8	災	wazawa(i), SAI	natural calamity	river, fire	4d3.3, 2206, 1448
A8	州	SHŪ	state, *province*	drop, drop, drop, river	2f4.1, 57, 99
A8	酬	SHŪ	compensation, reward	wine, province	7e6.2, 1539, 4785
A9	力	chikara, RYOKU, RIKI	power	grapheme	2g0.1, 3371, 715
A9	筋	suji, KIN	logic, muscle	bamboo, part of the body, power	6f6.4, 2678, 3395
A9	脅	obiya(kasu), odo(su), KYŌ	threaten	power, power, power, part of the body	2g8.2, 2109, 727
A10	刀	katana, TŌ	sword	grapheme	2f0.1, 2926, 665
A10	初	haji(me), hatsu, SHO	beginning, first	robe, sword	5e2.1, 1116, 4215
A10	辺	ata(ri), be, HEN	vicinity	sword, traveler	2q2.1, 3029, 4661
A10	刃	ha, JIN	*blade*	sword, drop	0a3.22, 2929, 152

A10	忍	shino(bu), NIN	*bear*, hide	blade, heart	4k3.3, 2212, 1684
A10	認	mito(meru), NIN	recognize, approve of	words, bear	7a7.10, 1546, 4370
A11	女	onna, NYO, JO	woman, feminine	grapheme	3e0.1, 3418, 1185
A11	安	yasu(i), AN	inexpensive, *peaceful*	house, woman	3m3.1, 2171, 1285
A11	案	AN	proposal, plan	peaceful, tree	3m7.6, 2270, 1308
A11	桜	sakura, Ō	cherry tree, cherry	tree, gather, woman	4a6.15, 931, 2256
A11	妥	DA	peace, depravity	caress, woman	3e4.9, 2400, 2823
A12	小	ko, chii(sai), SHŌ	small	grapheme	3n0.1, 7, 1355
A12	称	SHŌ	appellation, title	rice seedling, human, small	5d5.8, 1160, 3280
A13	少	suko(shi), suku(nai), SHŌ	little	grapheme	3n1.1, 3467, 166
A13	抄	SHŌ	excerpt	hand, little	3c4.11, 254, 1849

A13	秒	BYŌ	second	rice seedling, little	5d4.2, 1137, 3271
A13	妙	MYŌ	marvelous, strange	woman, little	3e4.5, 239, 1199
A13	砂	suna, SHA, SA	sand	stone, little	5a4.3, 1133, 3181
A13	劣	oto(ru), RETSU	inferior	little, power	3n3.4, 2395, 185
A14	皿	sara	plate	grapheme	5h0.1, 3474, 3113
A14	血	chi, KETSU	*blood*	drop, plate	5h1.1, 3526, 4205
A15	子	ko, SU, SHI	child	grapheme	2c0.1, 3390, 1264
A15	字	aza, JI	a section of a village character, letter	house, child	3m2.1, 2172, 1281
A15	好	su(ku), kono(mu), KŌ	like, favorable	woman, child	3e2.1, 208, 1191
A15	猛	MŌ	fierce	watchdog, child, plate	3g7.4, 537, 2895
A15	浮	u(ku), u(kareru), FU	float, be in high spirits	water, caress, child	3a6.11, 435, 2575

A16	母	haha, BO	mother	grapheme	0a5.36, 3475, 2466
A16	毎	MAI	*every*	human, mother	0a6.25, 2034, 2467
A16	海	umi, KAI	sea	water, every	3a6.20, 384, 2553
A16	悔	ku(yamu), kuya(shii), KAI	regret, repent of vexing	feeling, every	4k6.12, 365, 1682
A16	梅	ume, BAI	Japanese plum	tree, every	4a6.27, 925, 2258
A16	侮	anado(ru), BU	insult, despise	human being, every	2a6.20, 82, 421
A16	敏	BIN	agility, alertness	every, teacher	4i6.3, 1322, 2047
A17	父	chichi, FU	father	grapheme	2o2.3, 1973, 2832
A18	刈	ka(ru)	clip, cut	scissors, sword	2f2.1, 28, 666
A18	図	haka(ru), TO, ZU	plan, drawing	enclosed, drop, drop, scissors	3s4.3, 3071, 1034
A19	凶	KYŌ	bad luck, *evil*	scissors, container	0a4.19, 2961, 663

A19	悩	naya(mu/masu), NŌ	suffer (vi), afflict (vt)	feeling, gather, evil	4k7.11, 421, 1698
A19	脳	NŌ	brain	part of the body, gather, evil	4b7.7, 975, 3774
A20	斤	KIN	ax	grapheme	0a4.3, 2949, 2076
A20	近	chika(i), KIN	near, recent	ax, traveler	2q4.3, 3061, 4671
A20	祈	ino(ru), KI	pray	altar, ax	4e4.3, 875, 3234
A20	析	SEKI	analyze, cleave	wood, ax	4a4.12, 862, 2194
A20	折	o(reru/ru), SETSU	*break* (vi), bend (vt), fold	hand, ax	3c4.7, 253, 1855
A20	逝	yu(ku), SEI	pass away, die	break, traveler	2q7.8, 3104, 4691
A20	斥	SEKI	*expel*, reject	ax, drop	0a5.18, 2972, 175
A20	訴	utta(eru), SO	appeal to, sue	words, expel	7a5.2, 1507, 4340
A21	丘	oka, KYŪ	hill	grapheme	0a5.12, 3495, 174

A21	兵	HYŌ, HEI	*soldier*	hill, animal legs	2o5.6, 2551, 201
A21	浜	hama, HIN	beach	water, soldier	3a7.7, 436, 2567
A21	岳	take, GAKU	high mountain	hill, mountain	3o5.12, 2557, 208
A22	羽	ha, hane, U	feather, wing	grapheme	2b4.5, 226, 3673
B1	口	kuchi, KU, KŌ	mouth	grapheme	3d0.1, 3382, 868
B1	四	yon, yot(tsu), SHI	four	enclosed, legs	3s2.2, 3044, 1025
B1	回	mawa(ru/su), KAI	*turn around,* time	enclosed, mouth	3s3.1, 3055, 1028
B1	和	yawara(gu/geru), nago(mu), WA	soften, harmony, Japan	rice seedling, mouth	5d3.1, 1130, 3268
B1	如	NYO, JO	as, equal	woman, mouth	3e3.1, 207, 1189
B1	哲	TETSU	wisdom, philosophy	break, mouth	3d7.13, 2738, 931
B1	品	shina, HIN	*article*	mouth, mouth, mouth	3d6.15, 2248, 923

B1	器	utsuwa, KI	instrument, container	mouth, mouth, big, mouth, mouth	3d12.13, 2713, 994
B1	拐	KAI	kidnap	hand, mouth, sword	3c5.21, 308, 1865
B1	絹	kinu, KEN	silk	thread, mouth, part of the body	6a7.3, 1361, 3543
B1	塩	shio, EN	salt	earth, human, mouth, plate	3b10.4, 631, 1125
B2	言	i(u), koto, GON, GEN	say, words	grapheme	7a0.1, 1941, 4309
B2	信	SHIN	believe, trust	human being, words	2a7.1, 100, 454
B2	罰	BATSU, BACHI	punishment	net, words, sword	5g9.1, 2613, 3646
B2	誓	chika(u), SEI	swear, vow	break, words	7a7.17, 2754, 4369
B3	占	shi(meru), urana(u), SEN	occupy, divine, tell fortunes	grapheme	2m3.2, 2003, 799
B3	粘	neba(ru), NEN	be sticky	rice, divine	6b5.4, 1327, 3472
B3	店	mise, TEN	shop, store	building, divine	3q5.4, 3085, 1509

B3	点	TEN	point	divine, cooking fire	2m7.2, 2084, 804
B4	加	kuwa(waru/eru), KA	add	grapheme	2g3.1, 38, 716
B4	架	ka(karu/keru), KA	hang (vi, vt), lay across	add, wood	4a5.36, 2569, 2237
B5	召	me(su), SHŌ	summon (honorific)	grapheme	2f3.3, 2001, 668
B5	沼	numa, SHŌ	swamp	water, summon	3a5.24, 339, 2521
B5	招	mane(ku), SHŌ	invite	hand, summon	3c5.22, 316, 1882
B5	詔	mikotonori, SHŌ	imperial edict	words, summon	7a5.10, 1505, 4333
B5	紹	SHŌ	introduce	thread, summon	6a5.10, 135, 3516
B5	昭	SHŌ	luminous, *bright*	sun, summon	4c5.4, 894, 2114
B5	照	te(ru/rasu), SHŌ	illuminate	bright, cooking fire	4d9.12, 2827, 2785
B6	豆	mame, TŌ	bean	grapheme	3d4.22, 1943, 4465

B6	頭	atama, kashira, TŌ, ZU	head	bean, head	9a7.6, 1604, 4469
B6	痘	TŌ	small pox	sickness, bean	5i7.8, 3284, 3053
B7	兄	ani, KEI	older brother	grapheme	3d2.9, 2154, 875
B7	況	KYŌ	condition	water, older brother	3a5.21, 337, 2516
B7	祝	iwa(u), SHUKU	celebrate	altar, older brother	4e5.5, 913, 3244
B8	鋭	surudo(i), EI	sharp	metal, satan	8a7.12, 1730, 4864
B8	税	ZEI	tax	rice seedling, satan	5d7.4, 1191, 3287
B8	説	to(ku), SETSU	explain, persuade, theory	words, satan	7a7.12, 1547, 4373
B8	悦	ETSU	joy	feeling, satan	4k7.15, 418, 1696
B8	脱	nu(gu/gasu), DATSU	undress, remove, escape from	part of the body, satan	4b7.8, 973, 3775
B9	帥	SUI	commander in chief	chief, cloth	3f6.1, 1290, 109

B9	師	SHI	master, teacher	chief, one, cloth	3f7.2, 1326, 113
B9	追	o(u), TSUI	chase	chief, traveler	2q6.4, 3096, 4686
B10	官	KAN	*government*, government official	house, officer	3m5.6, 2226, 1295
B10	棺	KAN	coffin	wood, government	4a8.25, 985, 2298
B10	館	KAN	public building	eat, government	8b8.3, 1748, 5174
B10	管	kuda, KAN	pipe	bamboo, government	6f8.12, 2701, 3416
B11	宮	miya, GŪ, KYŪ	royal palace, Shinto shrine	house, management	3m7.5, 2274, 1310
B12	中	naka, CHŪ	middle, in, throughout	grapheme	0a4.40, 3451, 81
B12	仲	naka, CHŪ	personal relations, intermediary	human being, middle	2a4.7, 43, 378
B12	沖	oki, CHŪ	open sea	water, middle	3a4.5, 262, 2505
B12	忠	CHŪ	loyalty	middle, heart	4k4.6, 2433, 1653

B13	虫	mushi, CHŪ	insect	grapheme	6d0.1, 3530, 4115
B13	独	hito(ri), DOKU	alone, Germany	watchdog, insect	3g6.1, 395, 2884
B14	遣	tsuka(u/wasu), KEN	dispatch	middle course, officer, traveler	2q10.2, 3152, 4732
B15	患	wazura(u), KAN	be ill, suffer from	central point, heart	4k7.18, 2747, 1697
C1	日	hi, ka, JITSU, NICHI	day, sun	grapheme	4c0.1, 3027, 2097
C1	晶	SHŌ	crystal	sun, sun, sun	4c8.6, 2474, 2137
C1	唱	tona(eru), SHŌ	recite, chant	mouth, sun, sun	3d8.9, 462, 941
C1	宴	EN	banquet	house, sun, woman	3m7.3, 2271, 1304
C1	温	atata(maru/meru), atata(kai), ON	warm oneself (vi), warm (vt), warm	water, sun, plate	- 3a9.21, 608, 2634
C1	厚	atsu(i), KŌ	thick, kind	cliff, sun, child	2p6.1, 3003, 824
C2	担	katsu(gu), nina(u), TAN	bear on shoulder, undertake	hand, sunrise	3c5.20, 318, 1879

C2	胆	TAN	gallbladder	part of the body, sunrise	4b5.6, 919, 3751
C2	但	tada(shi)	but, provided that	human being, sunrise	2a5.14, 72, 394
C3	恒	KŌ	constant	feeling, period of time	4k6.5, 367, 1683
C3	垣	kaki	fence	earth, period of time	3b6.5, 351, 1075
C3	宣	SEN	proclamation	house, period of time	3m6.2, 2252, 1301
C4	旧	KYŪ	former	grapheme	4c1.1, 14, 94
C4	児	NI, JI	infant	former, legs	4c3.3, 2548, 572
C4	稲	ine, TŌ	rice plant	rice seedling, caress, former	5d9.2, 1219, 3294
C4	陥	ochii(ru)/, otoshii(reru), KAN	fall in, run into, entrap	fortress, tied up, former	2d7.11, 457, 4990
C5	白	shiro, shiro(i), BYAKU, HAKU	white	grapheme	4c1.3, 3493, 3095
C5	拍	HYŌ, HAKU	beat, clap the hands	hand, white	3c5.14, 304, 1872

C5	泊	to(maru/meru), HAKU	stay overnight (vi), lodge (vt)	water, white	3a5.15, 331, 2527
C5	伯	HAKU	count, eldest brother	human being, white	2a5.7, 59, 397
C5	迫	sema(ru), HAKU	press, draw near	white, traveler	2q5.5, 3074, 4676
C5	習	nara(u), SHŪ	learn	feather, white	4c7.11, 2667, 3675
C5	楽	tano(shii), RAKU, GAKU	*fun*, pleasant, comfortable, music	white, very much, tree	4a9.29, 2826, 2324
C5	薬	kusuri, YAKU	drug	flower, fun	3k13.15, 2375, 4074
C5	綿	wata, MEN	cotton	thread, white, cloth	6a8.8, 1373, 3566
C6	原	hara, GEN	plain, field, original	grapheme	2p8.1, 3009, 825
C6	源	minamoto, GEN	source	water, original	3a10.25, 656, 2656
C6	願	nega(u), GAN	wish, desire	original, head	3a10.2, 1845, 255
C7	百	HYAKU	hundred	grapheme	4c2.3, 2026, 33

C7	宿	yado(ru/su), yado, SHUKU	*lodge*, be pregnant, inn	house, human being, hundred	3m8.3, 2293, 1317
C7	縮	chiji(maru/meru), SHUKU	shrink, shorten	thread, lodge	6a11.9, 1414, 3608
C8	門	kado, MON	gate	grapheme	8e0.1, 888, 4940
C8	問	to(u), MON	question	gate, mouth	8e3.1, 3320, 4944
C8	聞	ki(ku), MON, BUN	hear, ask	gate, ear	8e6.1, 3326, 4959
C8	閲	ETSU	inspection, review	gate, satan	8e7.2, 3330, 4961
C8	間	aida, ma, KEN, KAN	between, among, *intermittent*	gate, sun	8e4.3, 3323, 4949
C8	簡	KAN	simple	bamboo, intermittent	6f12.5, 2721, 3444
C8	潤	uruo(u/su), JUN	moist, profit (vi), moisten (vt)	water, gate, king	3a12.20, 742, 2700
C9	根	ne, KON	root	tree, solid	4a6.5, 930, 2261
C9	恨	ura(mu), ura(meshii), KON	hold a grudge	feeling, solid	4k6.2, 369, 1677

C9	銀	GIN	silver	metal, solid	8a6.3, 1722, 4855
C9	限	kagi(ru), GEN	limit	fortress, solid	2d6.1, 398, 4987
C9	退	shirizo(ku/keru), TAI	retreat (vi), repel (vt)	solid, traveler	2q6.3, 3094, 4684
C9	即	SOKU	*immediate*	solid, seal	2e5.1, 1120, 3886
C9	節	fushi, SETSU	joint, knuckle, season, period	bamboo, immediate	6f7.3, 2691, 3402
C10	良	yo(i), RYŌ	good	grapheme	0a7.3, 3558, 3885
C10	浪	RŌ	waves, billows	water, good	3a7.5, 439, 2570
C10	朗	hoga(raka), RŌ	clear, bright	(good), moon	4b6.11, 1325, 3762
C10	郎	RŌ	*male name suffix*	(good), city wall	2d6.5, 1289, 4762
C10	廊	RŌ	corridor	building, male name suffix	3q8.4, 3147, 1519
C10	娘	musume	daughter	woman, good	3e7.2, 406, 1225

C11	鳥	tori, CHŌ	bird	bird, cooking fire	11b0.1, 3312, 5340
C11	鳴	na(ru/rasu), na(ku), MEI	sound, cry, chirp	mouth, bird, cooking fire	3d11.1, 674, 983
C11	島	shima, TŌ	island	bird, mountain	3o7.9, 3310, 230
C12	車	kuruma, SHA	vehicle, wheel	grapheme	3c0.1, 3552, 4608
C12	陣	JIN	battle, array, camp	fortress, vehicle	2d7.1, 455, 4992
C12	庫	KO	storage chamber	building, vehicle	3q7.1, 3112, 1512
C12	連	tsu(reru), REN, tsura(naru/neru)	take someone along, link	vehicle, traveler	2q7.2, 3103, 4702
C12	漸	ZEN	gradually	water, vehicle, ax	3a11.2, 706, 1680
C12	暫	ZAN	short while	vehicle, ax, sun	4c11.3, 2864, 2156
C13	目	me, MOKU	eye	grapheme	5c0.1, 3043, 3127
C13	眼	GAN	eye	eye, solid	5c6.1, 1172, 3140

C13	冒	oka(su), BŌ	*risk*, attack	sun, eye	4c5.6, 2434, 2117
C13	帽	BŌ	hat	cloth, risk	3f9.1, 568, 1483
C13	省	kaeri(miru), SEI, habu(ku), SHŌ	reflect upon, omit, ministry	little, eye	5c4.7, 2449, 218
C14	相	ai, SŌ, SHŌ	mutual, minister	grapheme	4a5.3, 900, 2241
C14	霜	shimo, SŌ	frost	rain, mutual	8d9.2, 2815, 5064
C14	想	SŌ	idea	mutual, heart	4k9.18, 2828, 1728
C14	箱	hako	box	bamboo, mutual	6f9.4, 2711, 3425
C15	且	ka(tsu)	additionally, furthermore	grapheme	0a5.15, 3485, 23
C15	租	SO	crop tax	rice seedling, additionally	5d5.7, 1161, 3279
C15	祖	SO	ancestor	altar, additionally	4e5.4, 914, 3243
C15	粗	ara(i), SO	coarse, rough	rice, additionally	6b5.2, 1329, 3473

C15	組	ku(mu), SO	assemble, group	thread, additionally	6a5.7, 1337, 3520
C15	阻	haba(mu), SO	obstruct separate from	fortress, additionally	2d5.1, 348, 4984
C15	助	tasu(karu/keru), JO	be helped (vi), help (vt)	additionally, power	2g5.1, 1121, 719
C15	宜	GI	all right	house, additionally	3m5.7, 2223, 1290
C15	査	SA	examine, look into	wood, additionally	4a5.32, 2437, 2235
C16	自	mizuka(ra), JI, SHI	self (graphem: nose)	grapheme	5c1.1, 3525, 3841
C16	息	iki, SOKU	*breath*, son	nose, heart	4k6.17, 2647, 3844
C16	臭	kusa(i), SHŪ	bad smell	nose, big	5c4.3, 2633, 3842
C17	首	kubi, SHU	neck, head	grapheme	2o7.2, 2265, 5186
C17	道	michi, DŌ	*way*	neck, traveler	2q9.14, 3134, 4724
C18	見	mi(ru), mi(seru), KEN	see, show	grapheme	5c2.1, 2544, 4284

C18	現	arawa(reru/su), GEN	appear, actual	king, see	4f7.3, 968, 2943
C18	視	SHI	regard, look at	altar, see	4e7.1, 972, 3248
C19	貝	kai	shellfish	grapheme	7b0.1, 2543, 4486
C19	敗	yabu(reru), HAI	be defeated	money, teacher	7b4.1, 1427, 4494
C19	買	ka(u), BAI	buy	net, money	5g7.2, 2598, 3637
C19	貫	tsuranu(ku), KAN	*penetrate*	mother, money	7b4.3, 2460, 2469
C19	慣	na(reru/rasu), KAN	get used to	feeling, penetrate	4k11.9, 685, 1756
C19	負	ma(keru/kasu), FU	lose (vi), defeat (vt)	tied up, money	2n7.1, 2091, 4488
C19	賀	GA	congratulation	add, money	7b5.10, 2599, 4501
C19	質	SHITSU, SHICHI	quality, pawn	ax, ax, money	7b8.7, 2808, 4518
C19	貴	tatto(i), KI	*noble*, your honorable	middle course, money	7b5.7, 2606, 4504

C19	遺	I, YUI	leave behind	noble, traveler	2q12.4, 3166, 4745
C19	賓	HIN	guest	house, one, little, money	3m12.3, 2357, 1339
C19	鎖	kusari, SA	chain	metal, small, money	8a10.2, 1761, 4901
C19	貞	TEI	*chastity*	divining rod, money	2m7.1, 2083, 803
C19	偵	TEI	spy	human being, chastity	2a9.15, 138, 502
C19	員	IN	*member*	mouth, money	3d7.10, 2269, 1979
C19	損	soko(nau/neru), SON	harm, loss	hand, member	3c10.12, 651, 4487
C20	則	SOKU	rule	grapheme	7b2.1, 1444, 4487
C20	側	kawa, SOKU	side	human being, rule	2a9.4, 137, 509
C20	測	haka(ru), SOKU	measure	water, rule	3a9.4, 610, 2632
D1	田	ta, DEN	rice field	grapheme	5f0.1, 3041, 2994

D1	畑	hata, hatake	field	fire, rice field	4d5.1, 905, 2757
D1	細	hoso(i), koma(kai), SAI	slender, narrow	thread, rice field	6a5.1, 1333, 3552
D1	思	omo(u), SHI	think	rice field, heart	5f4.4, 2564, 3001
D1	男	otoko, DAN, NAN	*man*	rice field, power	5f2.2, 2542, 2996
D1	勇	isa(mu), YŪ	be spirited, brave, encouraged	typical, man	2g7.3, 2089, 726
D1	胃	I	*stomach*	rice field, part of the body	5f4.3, 2561, 3000
D1	雷	kaminari, RAI	thunder	rain, rice field	8d5.1, 2791, 5049
D2	苗	nae, BYŌ	seedling	grapheme	3k5.2, 2237, 3923
D2	描	ega(ku), BYŌ	depict, draw	hand, seedling	3c8.21, 488, 1936
D2	猫	neko, BYŌ	cat	watchdog, seedling	3g8.5, 535, 2893
D3	富	to(mu), FU	be rich, wealth	house, prosperity	3m9.5, 2310, 1321

D3	福	FUKU	fortune	altar, prosperity	4e9.1, 1029, 3256
D3	副	FUKU	duplicate, assistant	prosperity, sword	2f9.2, 1776, 699
D3	幅	haba, FUKU	width	cloth, prosperity	3f9.2, 569, 1484
D4	魚	sakana, GYO	fish	grapheme	11a0.1, 2127, 5281
D4	漁	GYO, RYŌ	fishing	water, fish	3a11.1, 698, 2684
D5	増	fu(eru/yasu), ma(su), ZŌ	increase	earth, augment	3b11.3, 677, 1137
D5	憎	niku(mu), niku(i), ZŌ	hate, hateful	feeling, augment	4k11.7, 687, 1757
D5	贈	oku(ru), ZŌ	send, give to	money, augment	7b11.2, 1634, 4525
D5	僧	SŌ	monk	human being, augment	2a11.7, 159, 536
D6	由	yoshi, YU, YŪ	reason	grapheme	0a5.35, 2499, 89
D6	油	abura, YU	oil	water, reason	3a5.6, 341, 2534

D6	抽	CHŪ	draw out	hand, reason	3c5.7, 302, 1877
D6	宙	CHŪ	space, midair	house, reason	3m5.5, 2221, 1291
D6	軸	JIKU	axis	vehicle, reason	7c5.1, 1514, 4619
D6	笛	fue, TEKI	flute	bamboo, reason	6f5.6, 2664, 3382
D6	画	GA, KAKU	picture	one, reason, container	0a8.7, 3000, 50
D6	演	EN	performance	water, house, one, reason, animal legs	3a11.13, 697, 2685
D7	恵	megu(mu), KEI, E	*bless* grace, favor	alms, heart	4k6.16, 2659, 1681
D7	穂	ho, SUI	ear/head of grain	rice seedling, bless	5d10.2, 1232, 3300
D8	曲	ma(garu/geru), KYOKU	bend, curve, musical composition	grapheme	0a6.27, 3527, 103
D8	豊	yuta(ka), HŌ	plentiful	bend, bean	3d10.15, 2697, 4466
D8	典	TEN	law code	(bend), animal legs	2o6.5, 2627, 588

D9	曹	SŌ	comrade, sergeant	grapheme	4c7.10, 2746, 2134
D9	遭	a(u), SŌ	meet with, encounter	comrade, traveler	2q11.2, 3159, 4736
D9	槽	SŌ	water tank	wood, comrade	4a11.7, 1067, 2351
D10	甲	KŌ, KAN	first in a series, shell	grapheme	0a5.34, 3481, 92
D10	押	o(su), Ō	push	hand, first in a series	3c5.5, 314, 1885
D10	岬	misaki	cape	mountain, first in a series	3o5.4, 284, 1412
D11	申	mō(su), SHIN	speak humbly, report	grapheme	0a5.39, 3507, 93
D11	伸	no(biru/basu), SHIN	stretch	human being, report	2a5.3, 70, 403
D11	神	kami, SHIN, JIN	god	altar, report	4e5.1, 912, 3245
D11	紳	SHIN	gentleman	thread, report	6a5.2, 1334, 3518
D12	里	sato, RI	countryside	grapheme	0a7.9, 3542, 4813

D12	理	RI	reason, principle	king, countryside	4f7.1, 970, 2942
D12	厘	RIN	very small	cliff, countryside	2p7.1, 3004, 823
D12	埋	u(maru/meru), MAI	bury	earth, countryside	3b7.2, 403, 1084
D12	黒	kuro, kuro(i), KOKU	*black*	countryside, cooking fire	4d7.2, 2740, 5403
D12	墨	sumi, BOKU	ink	black, earth	3b11.4, 2753, 5404
D12	量	haka(ru), RYŌ	measure, *quantity*	sunrise, countryside	4c8.9, 2471, 2141
D12	糧	kate, RYŌ	food, provisions	rice, quantity	6b12.1, 1421, 3490
D13	単	TAN	single	grapheme	3n6.2, 2256, 139
D13	弾	hazu(mu), hi(ku), tama, DAN	spring back, play an instrument, projectile	bow, single	3h9.3, 572, 1575
D13	禅	ZEN	Zen-Buddhism	altar, single	4e9.2, 1032, 3255
D14	果	ha(teru/tasu), KA	end (vi), carry out (vt), fruit	grapheme	0a8.8, 3560, 107

D14	菓	KA	cake, fruit	flower, fruit	3k8.2, 2302, 3980
D14	課	KA	lesson, section	words, fruit	7a8.2, 1573, 4389
D14	裸	hadaka, RA	naked	robe, fruit	5e8.1, 1211, 4248
D14	巣	su, SŌ	nest	gather, fruit	3n8.1, 2295, 141
E1	丁	CHŌ, TEI	block of houses	grapheme	0a2.4, 3348, 2
E1	町	machi, CHŌ	town, quarter	rice field, block of houses	5f2.1, 1113, 2995
E1	庁	CHŌ	government agency	building, block of houses	3q2.2, 3034, 1498
E1	頂	itada(ku), itadaki, CHŌ	receive humbly, summit	block of houses, head	9a2.1, 145, 5118
E1	貯	CHO	savings	money, house, block of houses	7b5.1, 1509, 4502
E1	打	u(tsu), DA	strike	hand, block of houses	3c2.3, 193, 1929
E1	灯	hi, TŌ	lamp	fire, block of houses	4d2.1, 825, 2745

E1	訂	TEI	revision	words, block of houses	7a2.3, 1442, 4310
E1	寧	NEI	courteous	house, heart, net, block of houses	3m11.8, 2345, 1335
E2	了	RYŌ	finish	grapheme	2c0.3, 3350, 268
E2	予	YO	*in advance*	typical, finish	0a4.12, 1983, 271
E2	預	azu(karu/keru), YO	deposit	in advance, head	9a4.5, 1042, 5123
E2	序	JO	beginning, preface	building, in advance	3q4.4, 3065, 1502
E2	野	no, YA	field	countryside, in advance	0a11.5, 1485, 4814
E3	矛	hoko, MU	halberd	grapheme	0a5.6, 2008, 3164
E3	務	tsuto(meru), MU	*make efforts*, duty	halberd, teacher, power	4i7.6, 1173, 3767
E3	霧	kiri, MU	fog	rain, make efforts	8d11.1, 2817, 5065
E3	柔	yawa(raka), JŪ, NYŪ	soft	halberd, wood	4a5.34, 2088, 3166

E4	可	KA	possibility, approval	grapheme	3d2.12, 2969, 24
E4	河	kawa, KA	river	water, possibility	3a5.30, 336, 2530
E4	何	nani, KA	*what*, how many	human being, possibility	2a5.21, 65, 409
E4	荷	ni, KA	baggage	flower, what	3k7.10, 2282, 3956
E5	奇	KI	unusual	grapheme	3d5.17, 2217, 1176
E5	寄	yo(ru/seru), KI	draw near	house, unusual	3m8.8, 2291, 1318
E5	騎	KI	ride on horseback	horse, unusual	10a8.3, 1834, 5222
E5	崎	saki	steep, cape	mountain, unusual	3o8.3, 466, 1426
E6	芽	me, GA	sprout, spear	flower, tusk	3k5.9, 2240, 3920
E6	雅	GA	elegant	tusk, chicken	8c5.1, 1197, 2850
E6	邪	JA	evil	tusk, city wall	2d5.8, 1124, 2849

E7	示	shime(su), JI, SHI	show	grapheme	4e0.1, 1936, 3228
E7	宗	SŌ, SHŪ	*religion*	house, show	3m5.1, 2228, 1294
E7	崇	SŪ	revere	mountain, religion	308.9, 2297, 1429
E8	芋	imo	potato	flower, expanse	3k3.1, 2181, 3896
E8	宇	U	universe	house, expanse	3m3.3, 2175, 1280
E8	呼	yo(bu), KO	call	mouth, (expanse), drop, drop	3d5.4, 273, 914
E9	才	SAI	talent	grapheme	0a3.27, 3410, 270
E9	材	ZAI	timber, material	wood, talent	4a3.7, 836, 2189
E9	財	ZAI	financial wealth	money, talent	7b3.1, 1457, 4490
E9	閉	to(jiru/zasu), shi(maru/meru),HEI	close	gate, talent	8e3.3, 3319, 4945
E10	寸	SUN	approx. 3 cm, a bit of	grapheme	0a3.17, 2935, 1348

E10	村	mura, SON	village	tree, a bit of	4a3.11, 834, 2191
E10	討	u(tsu), TŌ	attack, study	words, a bit of	7a3.3, 1456, 4316
E10	団	DAN	group	enclosed, a bit of	3s3.3, 3053, 1027
E10	守	mamo(ru), SHU	*protect*, abide by	house, a bit of	3m3.2, 2173, 1282
E10	狩	ka(ru), ka(ri), SHU	hunt	watchdog, protect	3g6.5, 397, 2883
E10	闘	tataka(u), TŌ	fight	gate, bean, a bit of	8e10.2, 3334, 4973
E10	爵	SHAKU	rank of nobility	caress, net, (solid), a bit of	5g12.1, 2524, 2830
E10	将	SHŌ	*general officer*	bed, caress, a bit of	2b8.3, 460, 2840
E10	奨	SHŌ	encourage	general officer, big	3n10.4, 2842, 1181
E10	導	michibi(ku), DŌ	guide	way, a bit of	5c9.3, 2888, 1354
E10	奪	uba(u), DATSU	rob	big, chicken, a bit of	8c6.4, 2343, 1183

E11	付	tsu(ku/keru), FU	be attached, attach	grapheme	2a3.6, 31, 363
E11	附	FU	accompany, appendix	fortress, attach	2d5.4, 347, 4983
E11	符	FU	symbol	bamboo, attach	6f5.12, 2661, 3383
E11	府	FU	*urban prefecture*	building, attach	3q5.2, 3082, 1507
E12	寺	tera, JI	Buddhist temple	grapheme	3b3.5, 2164, 1054
E12	時	toki, JI	time	sun, Buddhist temple	4c6.2, 924, 2126
E12	侍	samurai, JI	samurai	human being, Buddhist temple	2a6.11, 85, 427
E12	持	mo(tsu), JI	hold	hand, Buddhist temple	3c6.8, 374, 1903
E12	詩	SHI	poetry	words, Buddhist temple	7a6.5, 1524, 4360
E12	等	hito(shii), TŌ	equal, class	bamboo, Buddhist temple	6f6.9, 2682, 3396
E13	専	moppa(ra), SEN	exclusive	grapheme	0a9.16, 2644, 1350

E13	博	HAKU	specialist, extensive	ten, exclusive, drop	2k10.1, 151, 787
E13	薄	usu(i), HAKU	thin	flower, water, exclusive, drop	3k13.11, 2370, 4075
E13	縛	shiba(ru), BAKU	bind	thread, exclusive, drop	6a10.3, 1405, 3593
E13	簿	BO	record book	bamboo, water, exclusive, drop	6f13.4, 2727, 3448
F1	十	tō, JŪ	ten	grapheme	2k0.1, 3365, 768
F1	汁	shiru, JŪ	soup, juice	water, ten	3a2.1, 195, 2485
F1	計	haka(rau), haka(ru), KEI	arrange, compute, plan	words, ten	7a2.1, 1441, 4312
F1	針	hari, SHIN	needle	metal, ten	8a2.3, 1666, 4817
F1	協	KYŌ	cooperation	ten, power, power, power	2k6.1, 93, 774
F1	聴	ki(ku), CHŌ	listen	ear, ten, net, heart	6e11.3, 1418, 3716
F2	斗	TO	bucket with approx. 18 liters	grapheme	8e10.2, 2953, 2073

F2	料	RYŌ	fee, materials	rice seedling, bucket	6b4.4, 1292, 3468
F2	科	KA	department, faculty	rice, bucket	5d4.3, 1138, 3272
F2	叫	sake(bu), KYŌ	shout	mouth, (bucket)	3d3.4, 201, 881
F2	糾	KYŪ	twist (a rope)	thread, (bucket)	6a3.4, 1278, 3498
F2	卑	iya(shimu), iya(shii), HI	*despise*, mean	drop, rice field, (bucket)	5f4.8, 2642, 221
F2	碑	HI	tombstone	stone, despise	5a9.2, 1213, 3206
F3	古	furu(i), KO	old	grapheme	2k3.1, 2002, 770
F3	枯	ka(reru/rasu), KO	wither, let wither	tree, old	4a5.26, 898, 2238
F3	故	yue, KO	old, the late	old, teacher	4i5.2, 1141, 2044
F3	湖	mizuumi, KO	lake	water, old, moon	3a9.8, 604, 2628
F3	苦	kuru(shimu/shimeru),niga(i),KU	suffer (vi), torment (vt), bitter	flower, old	3k5.24, 2243, 3928

F3	克	KOKU	overcome	old, legs	2k5.1, 2046, 772
F4	固	kata(i), KO	hard, firm	grapheme	3s5.2, 2086, 1036
F4	個	KO	individual, general counter	human being, hard	2a8.36, 117, 489
F4	箇	KA	counter for things or places	bamboo, hard	6f8.15, 2700, 3414
F5	早	haya(i), SŌ	early, quick	grapheme	4c2.1, 2390, 2100
F5	草	kusa, SŌ	grass	flower, early	3k6.13, 2263, 3939
F5	卓	TAKU	*prominent*, table	divining rod, early	2m6.2, 2064, 802
F5	悼	ita(mu), TŌ	mourn	feeling, prominent	4k8.13, 485, 1706
F6	朝	asa, CHŌ	*morning*	fog, moon	4b8.12, 1695, 3788
F6	潮	shio, CHŌ	tide	water, morning	3a12.1, 739, 2702
F7	干	ho(su), KAN	dry	grapheme	2k1.1, 3379, 1492

F7	刊	KAN	publication	dry, sword	2f3.1, 190, 1493
F7	汗	ase, KAN	sweat	water, dry	3a3.6, 220, 2493
F7	肝	kimo, KAN	liver	part of the body, dry	4b3.2, 841, 3731
F7	軒	noki, KEN	eaves, counter for houses	vehicle, dry	7c3.1, 1459, 4611
F7	岸	kishi, GAN	shore	mountain, cliff, dry	3o5.11, 2236, 1413
F7	幸	saiwa(i), sachi, shiawa(se), KŌ	*happiness*, happy	earth, drop, drop, dry	3b5.9, 2216, 1073
F8	謡	uta(u), YŌ	sing	words, vibrate	7a9.9, 1597, 4410
F8	揺	yu(reru), YŌ	shake	hand, vibrate	3c9.8, 594, 1965
F9	平	hira, tai(ra), HEI, BYŌ	flat, ordinary	grapheme	2k3.4, 3478, 26
F9	評	HYŌ	comment	words, flat	7a5.3, 150, 4339
F9	坪	tsubo	unit of square measure, 3.3 sq.m.	earth, flat	3b5.4, 275, 1072

F10	羊	hitsuji, YŌ	sheep	grapheme	2o4.1, 2183, 3656
F10	洋	YŌ	ocean, Western	water, sheep	3a6.19, 392, 2550
F10	詳	kuwa(shii), SHŌ	detailed	words, sheep	7a6.12, 1526, 4357
F10	祥	SHŌ	happiness	altar, sheep	4e6.1, 948, 3246
F10	鮮	aza(yaka), SEN	fresh, vivid	fish, sheep	11a6.7, 1877, 5295
F10	達	TATSU	attain	earth, sheep, traveler	2q9.8, 3139, 4721
F10	拝	oga(mu), HAI	worship, pray to	hand, (sheep), one	3c5.3, 303, 1884
F11	半	naka(ba), HAN	half	grapheme	0a5.24, 3501, 132
F11	伴	tomona(u), HAN, BAN	accompany	human being, half	2a5.4, 60, 396
F11	畔	HAN	ridge between rice paddies	rice field, half	5f5.1, 1145, 3002
F11	判	HAN, BAN	judge	half, sword	2f5.2, 1122, 673

F12	年	toshi, NEN	year	human, barrier	0a6.16, 2035, 188
F13	偉	era(i), I	great, famous	human being, thief	2a10.5, 148, 506
F13	緯	I	latitude	thread, thief	6a10.7, 1407, 3579
F13	違	chiga(u), I	differ	thief, traveler	2q10.5, 3151, 4720
G1	千	chi, SEN	thousand	grapheme	2k1.2, 3411, 156
G2	舌	shita, ZETSU	tongue	grapheme	3d3.9, 2186, 3855
G2	活	KATSU	active, live	water, tongue	3a6.16, 385, 2552
G2	括	KATSU	lump together	hand, tongue	3c6.12, 376, 1896
G2	話	hana(su), WA	speak	words, tongue	7a6.8, 1527, 4358
G2	憩	iko(u), KEI	take a rest	tongue, breath	4k12.10, 2890, 1765
G3	重	kasa(naru/neru), omo(i), JŪ, CHŌ	duplicate, heavy, -fold	grapheme	0a9.18, 3573, 224

G3	動	ugo(ku/kasu), DŌ	*move* (vi, vt)	heavy, power	2g9.1, 1778, 730
G3	働	hatara(ku), DŌ	work	human being, move	2a11.1, 153, 532
G3	勳	KUN	merit	move, cooking fire	4d11.3, 2869, 2794
G3	薫	kao(ru), KUN	smell, be fragrant	flower, heavy, cooking fire	3k13.17, 2371, 4073
G3	種	tane, SHU	seed, variety	rice seedling, heavy	5d9.1, 1218, 3295
G3	挿	sa(su), SŌ	insert	hand, (thousand), first in a series	3c7.2, 431, 1916
G4	香	kao(ru), kao(ri), ka, KŌ	smell good, perfume	rice seedling, sun	5d4.5, 2568, 5188
G4	季	KI	season	rice seedling, child	5d2.3, 2554, 3266
G4	委	I	entrust	rice seedling, woman	5d3.2, 2553, 3267
G4	菌	KIN	bacteria	flower, enclosed, rice seedling	3k8.32, 2304, 3976
G4	利	ki(ku), RI	take effect *profit*	rice seedling, sword	5d2.1, 1114, 3264

G4	痢	RI	diarrhea	sickness, profit	5i7.2, 3283, 3049
G5	番	BAN	numerical order, watch	number, rice field	5f7.4, 2748, 4811
G5	藩	HAN	feudal domain	flower, water, number, rice field	3k15.4, 2379, 4089
G5	翻	hirugae(ru/su), HON	turn over, reverse	number, rice field, feather	6b12.3, 1897, 3681
G5	審	SHIN	trial, investigation	house, number, rice field	3m12.1, 2360, 1341
G6	任	maka(su), NIN	leave to, *duty*	human being, porter	2a4.9, 53, 374
G6	妊	NIN	pregnancy	woman, porter	3e4.3, 240, 1197
G6	賃	CHIN	charges, wage	duty, money	7b6.6, 2694, 4509
G7	廷	TEI	court	grapheme	2q4.2, 3058, 1546
G7	庭	niwa, TEI	garden	building, court	3q6.3, 3114, 1514
G8	手	te, SHU	hand, occupation suffix	grapheme	3c0.1, 3456, 1827

G8	看	KAN	watch, care for	(hand), eye	5c4.4, 3220, 222
G9	乗	no(ru/seru), JŌ	ride, get on	grapheme	0a9.19, 3576, 223
G9	剰	JŌ	surplus	ride, sword	2f9.1, 1779, 698
G10	垂	ta(reru/rasu), SUI	hang down (vi, vt)	grapheme	0a8.12, 3565, 211
G10	睡	SUI	sleep	eye, hang down	5c8.2, 1200, 3149
G10	錘	SUI	spindle	metal, hang down	8a8.2, 1744, 4872
G10	郵	YŪ	mail	hang down, city wall	2d8.12, 1687, 4768
G11	待	ma(tsu), TAI	wait	step, Buddhist temple	3i6.4, 264, 1609
G11	得	u(ru), e(ru), TOKU	acquire, gain	step, sunrise, a bit of	3i8.4, 477, 1622
G11	徳	TOKU	virtue	step, ten, net, heart	3i11.3, 684, 1633
G12	行	yu(ku), okona(u), KŌ, GYŌ	go, act	grapheme	3i3.1, 212, 4213

G12	衝	SHŌ	collision	heavy, (go)	3i12.1, 725, 1638
G12	衡	KŌ	balance	tied up, rice field, big, (go)	3i13.1, 761, 1641
G12	衛	EI	guard	thief, (go)	3i13.3, 760, 1639
G13	升	masu, SHŌ	bottle with approx. 1.8 liter	grapheme	0a4.32, 3455, 160
G13	昇	nobo(ru), SHŌ	ascend	sun, bottle	4c4.5, 2415, 2109
G14	准	JUN	quasi-, semi-	ice, chicken	2b8.1, 127, 648
G14	準	JUN	standard	water, chicken, ten	2k11.1, 2856, 791
G14	催	moyō(su), SAI	hold an event, sponsor	hermit, chicken	2a11.12, 157, 533
G14	唯	YUI	only	mouth, chicken	3d8.1, 463, 942
G14	推	o(su), SUI	infer, recommend	hand, chicken	3c8.1, 504, 1950
G14	稚	CHI	childish	rice seedling, chicken	5d8.1, 1206, 3292

G14	焦	ko(geru/gasu),SHŌ ase(ru),ko(gareru)	*scorch* (vi, vt), be impatient, pine for	chicken, cooking fire	3c4.3, 2770, 5029
G14	礁	SHŌ	reef	stone, scorch	5d12.2, 1243, 3220
G14	進	susu(mu/meru), SHIN	advance (vi, vt)	chicken, traveler	2q8.1, 3121, 4709
G14	集	atsu(maru/meru), tsudo(u), SHŪ	gather, collect	chicken, tree	8c4.2, 2771, 5031
G14	誰	dare	who	words, chicken	7a8.1, 1578, 4384
G14	確	tashi(kameru), tashi(ka), KAKU	ascertain, certain	stone, (one), chicken	5a10.3, 1228, 3217
H1	牛	ushi, GYŪ	cattle	grapheme	4g0.1, 3452, 2852
H1	件	KEN	matter	human being, cattle	2a4.4, 51, 368
H1	牧	maki, BOKU	pasture	cattle, teacher	4g4.1, 873, 2856
H1	特	TOKU	special, especially	cattle, Buddhist temple	2g6.1, 945, 2860
H1	制	SEI	*system*	cattle, (cloth), sword	2f6.1, 1274, 683

H2	告	tsu(geru), KOKU	notify	grapheme	3d4.18, 2409, 900
H2	酷	KOKU	severe, cruel	wine, notify	7e7.1, 1562, 4788
H2	造	tsuku(ru), ZŌ	produce, make	notify, traveler	2q7.11, 3110, 4701
H3	先	saki, SEN	ahead, earlier, destination	grapheme	3b3.7, 2394, 571
H3	洗	ara(u), SEN	wash	water, earlier	3a6.12, 388, 2551
H3	銑	SEN	pig iron	metal, earlier	3a6.4, 1726, 4850
H4	生	i(kiru/kasu), SEI, u(mareru/mu), SHŌ	live, be alive, bring to life	grapheme	0a5.29, 3497, 2991
H4	性	SEI, SHŌ	nature, sex	feeling, life	4k5.4, 299, 1666
H4	姓	SEI, SHŌ	surname	woman, life	3e5.3, 279, 1203
H4	星	hoshi, SEI, SHŌ	star	sun, life	4c5.7, 2435, 2121
H4	牲	SEI	sacrifice	cattle, life	4g5.1, 907, 2858

H5	朱	SHU	vermilion	grapheme	0a6.13, 3531, 184
H5	珠	SHU	pearl	king, vermilion	4f6.2, 947, 2936
H5	株	kabu	stub, stock	tree, vermilion	4a6.3, 935, 2257
H6	失	ushina(u), SHITSU	lose	grapheme	0a5.28, 3511, 178
H6	秩	CHITSU	order	rice seedling, lose	5d5.2, 1158, 3276
H6	鉄	TETSU	iron	metal, lose	8d5.6, 1711, 4844
H6	迭	TETSU	alternate	lose, traveler	2q5.2, 3077, 4672
H7	矢	ya, SHI	arrow	grapheme	0a5.19, 2009, 3168
H7	疾	SHITSU	disease, fast	sickness, arrow	5i5.12, 3279, 3041
H7	短	mijika(i), TAN	short	arrow, bean	3d9.27, 1182, 3172
H7	侯	KŌ	*feudal lord*	human being, ..., arrow	2a7.21, 98, 443

H7	候	KŌ	season, weather	halve, feudal lord	2a8.10, 119, 481
H7	知	shi(ru), CHI	*know*	arrow, mouth	3d5.14, 1127, 3169
H7	痴	CHI	foolish	sickness, know	5i8.1, 3286, 3061
H8	午	GO	noon	grapheme	2k2.2, 1984, 162
H8	許	yuru(su), KYO	permit	words, noon	7a4.3, 1470, 4324
H8	缶	KAN	*can*, tin	noon, container	2k4.6, 2033, 3634
H9	勧	susu(meru), KAN	encourage, recommend	eagle, power	2g11.1, 1857, 736
H9	観	KAN	view	eagle, see	5c13.7, 1880, 4296
H9	権	KEN, GON	right, power	tree, eagle	4a11.18, 1065, 2360
H10	作	tsuku(ru), SAKU, SA	make, work	human being, generate	2a5.10, 68, 407
H10	昨	SAKU	yesterday, last	sun, generate	4c5.3, 893, 2119

H10	酢	su, SAKU	vinegar	wine, generate	7e5.3, 1516, 4783
H10	詐	SA	lie, falsify	words, generate	7a5.6, 1502, 4337
H11	竹	take, CHIKU	bamboo	grapheme	6f0.1, 228, 3366
I1	士	SHI	scholar, profession suffix	grapheme	3p0.1, 2405, 1160
I1	仕	tsuka(eru), SHI	serve	human being, scholar	2a3.2, 34, 362
I1	志	kokoroza(su), SHI	aim, *ambition*	scholar, heart	3p4.1, 2199, 1064
I1	誌	SHI	magazine	words, ambition	7a7.8, 1548, 4366
I1	壮	SŌ	*vigorous*	bed, scholar	2b4.2, 224, 2837
I1	荘	SŌ	dignified, villa	flower, vigorous	3k6.12, 2262, 3938
I2	吉	KICHI, KITSU	good luck	grapheme	3p3.1, 2167, 1053
I2	詰	tsu(maru/meru), KITSU	closely packed (vi), press into (vt)	words, good luck	7a6.7, 1521, 4359

I2	結	musu(bu), yu(u), KETSU	tie, bind, do up (the hair)	thread, good luck	6a6.5, 1348, 3540
I2	喜	yoroko(bu), KI	be happy	good luck, horns, mouth	3p9.1, 2308, 1115
I2	樹	JU	tree, wood	tree, good luck, horns, a bit of	4a12.3, 1075, 2377
I2	膨	fuku(ramu), BŌ	swell out	part of the body, good luck, horns, style	4b12.1, 1084, 3818
I3	土	tsuchi, DO, TO	soil	grapheme	3b0.1, 3403, 1050
I3	吐	ha(ku), TO	spew, vomit	mouth, earth	3d3.1, 203, 883
I3	社	yashiro, SHA	Shinto shrine, company, society	altar, earth	4e3.1, 840, 3231
I3	圧	ATSU	pressure	cliff, earth	2p3.1, 2970, 818
I3	粧	SHŌ	makeup	rice, building, earth	6b6.1, 1345, 3475
I3	塁	RUI	(baseball) base, rampart	rice field, very much, earth	5f7.2, 2593, 3009
I3	陸	RIKU	mainland	fortress, earth, legs, earth	2d8.4, 543, 5005

I4	赤	aka(ramu), aka(i), aka, SEKI, SHAKU	become red, red	grapheme	3b4.10, 2193, 4534
I4	赦	SHA	amnesty	red, teacher	4i7.3, 1478, 4536
I4	嚇	KAKU	intimidate	mouth, red, red	3d14.1, 784, 1009
I5	佳	KA	excellent	human being, heap of earth	2a6.10, 86, 429
I5	涯	GAI	shore	water, cliff, heap of earth	3d8.33, 512, 2584
I5	街	machi, GAI	city quarter	heap of earth, go	3i9.2, 576, 1626
I5	掛	ka(karu/keru)	cost, hang	hand, heap of earth, divining rod	3c8.6, 493, 1952
I5	封	FŪ, HŌ	seal	heap of earth, a bit of	3b6.13, 1287, 1349
I6	孝	KŌ	filial piety	grapheme	2k4.3, 3196, 773
I6	酵	KŌ	ferment	wine, filial piety	7e6.1, 1561, 4787
I6	教	oso(waru)/oshi(eru) KYŌ	be taught (vi), teach (vt)	filial piety, teacher	4i6.1, 1493, 2952

I7	者	mono, SHA	(working) person	grapheme	4c4.13, 3211, 3685
I7	煮	ni(eru/ru), SHA	boil	working person, cooking fire	4d8.9, 2785, 2771
I7	都	miyako, TO, TSU	metropolis	working person, city wall	2d8.13, 1686, 4769
I7	諸	SHO	various	words, working person	7a8.3, 1577, 4393
I7	緒	SHO, CHO	outset	thread, working person	6a8.3, 1378, 3557
I7	署	SHO	government office	net, working person	5g8.1, 2609, 3642
I7	暑	atsu(i), SHO	hot, warm, summer heat	sun, working person	4c8.5, 2473, 2138
I7	著	arawa(su), ichijiru(shii), CHO	publish, remarkable	flower, working person	3k8.4, 2300, 3983
I8	工	KŌ, KU	handicraft, manufacture	grapheme	0a3.6, 3381, 1451
I8	紅	kurenai, beni, KŌ	crimson	thread, handicraft	6a3.6, 1277, 3500
I8	功	KŌ	merit	handicraft, power	2g3.2, 189, 1454

I8	貢	mitsu(gu), KŌ	support tribute	handicraft, money	7b3.3, 2281, 1458
I8	江	e, KŌ	bay	water, handicraft	3a3.8, 221, 2491
I8	項	KŌ	clause	handicraft, head	9a3.1, 567, 1459
I8	攻	se(meru), KŌ	attack	handicraft, teacher	4i3.2, 242, 1457
I9	五	itsu(tsu), GO	five	grapheme	0a4.27, 3436, 15
I9	悟	sato(ru), GO	awake to	feeling, five, mouth	4k7.5, 419, 1700
I9	語	kata(ru), GO	tell, language, word	words, five, mouth	7a7.6, 1543, 4374
I10	並	nara(bu/beru), nami, HEI	line up (vi, vt), ordinary	grapheme	2o6.1, 2246, 589
I10	普	FU	*widespread*	line up, sun	2o10.5, 2323, 605
I10	譜	FU	music, note, genealogy	words, widespread	7a12.2, 1637, 4437
I10	霊	tama, REI, RYŌ	soul, spirit	rain, two, line up	8d7.2, 2805, 5056

I10	湿	shime(ru/su), SHITSU	get damp, dampen	water, sun, line up	3d9.22, 609, 2631
I10	顕	KEN	obvious	sun, line up, head	9a9.5, 1806, 5137
I11	亜	A	Asia, sub-	grapheme	0a7.14, 3540, 43
I11	悪	waru(i), AKU, O	bad	Asia, heart	4k7.17, 2745, 62
I12	西	nishi, SEI, SAI	west (see N7)	grapheme	0a6.20, 3520, 4273
I12	価	atai, KA	price, value	human being, west	2a6.3, 87, 422
I12	煙	kemu(ri), EN	smoke	fire, west, earth	4d9.3, 1021, 2784
I12	要	i(ru), YŌ	*require*, necessity	west, woman	3e6.11, 2635, 4274
I12	腰	koshi, YŌ	waist	part of the body, require	4b9.3, 1036, 3799
I12	票	HYŌ	vote, *slip*	west, show	4e6.2, 2449, 4276
I12	漂	tadayo(u), HYŌ	drift	water, slip	3a11.9, 699, 2678

I12	標	HYŌ	mark, sign	wood, slip	4a11.8, 1064, 2359
I13	毒	DOKU	poison	cultivate, mother	0a8.14, 2428, 2468
I13	契	chigi(ru), KEI	*promise*, pledge	cultivate, sword, big	2f7.6, 2639, 1177
I13	喫	KITSU	consume	mouth, promise	3d9.7, 551, 961
I13	憲	KEN,	constitution	house, cultivate, net, heart	3m13.2, 2368, 1342
I13	害	GAI	*harm*	house, cultivate, mouth	3m7.4, 2272, 1306
I13	割	wa(reru/ru), wari sa(ku), KATSU	divide, crack, proportion, 10percent	harm, sword	2f10.1, 1816, 703
I13	轄	KATSU	wedge, administration	vehicle, harm	7c10.1, 1627, 4636
I14	謹	tsutsushi(mu), KIN	be respectful	words, inferior	7a10.6, 1618, 4424
I14	勤	tsuto(maru/meru), KIN	be fit for a task, hold a job	inferior, power	2g10.1, 1818, 732
I15	青	ao, ao(i), SEI	blue, youthful	grapheme	4b4.10, 2420, 5076

I15	清	kiyo(i), SEI	clear	water, blue	3a8.18, 523, 2605
I15	晴	ha(reru/rasu), SEI	clear up, blue sky	sun, blue	4c8.2, 981, 2145
I15	請	ko(u), u(keru), SEI	request, receive	words, blue	7a8.8, 1576, 4390
I15	精	SEI, SHŌ	spirit, vitality	rice, blue	6b8.1, 1366, 3480
I15	情	nasa(ke), JŌ, SEI	compassion	feeling, blue	4k8.9, 482, 1714
I16	責	se(meru), SEKI	blame, responsibility	grapheme	7b4.4, 2467, 4492
I16	積	tsu(moru/mu), SEKI	accumulate	rice seedling, responsibility	5d11.5, 1236, 3306
I16	績	SEKI	achievement	thread, responsibility	6a11.8, 1412, 3602
I16	漬	tsu(karu/keru)	immerse	water, responsibility	3a11.12, 702, 2676
I16	債	SAI	debt, bond	human being, responsibility	2a11.11, 156, 531
I17	王	Ō	king	grapheme	4f0.1, 3439, 2922

I17	皇	KŌ, Ō	emperor	white, king	4f5.9, 2566, 3100
I17	呈	TEI	*present*, gift	mouth, king	3d4.14, 2189, 895
I17	程	hodo, TEI	limits, extent degree	rice seedling, present	5d7.2, 1190, 3285
I17	狂	kuru(u), KYŌ	become mad, crazy	watchdog, king	3g4.2, 269, 2872
I17	聖	SEI	holy	ear, mouth, king	4f9.9, 2830, 2960
I17	徴	CHŌ	*levy*, symptom	step, mountain, king, teacher	3i11.2, 683, 1634
I17	懲	ko(riru/rashimeru), CHŌ	learn by experience	levy, heart	4k14.3, 2910, 1785
I17	玉	tama, GYOKU	*gem*, ball jewel	king, drop	4f0.2, 3477, 2923
I17	宝	takara, HŌ	treasure	house, gem	3m5.2, 2224, 1293
I17	国	kuni, KOKU	country	enclosed, gem	3s5.1, 3087, 1037
I18	主	nushi, omo, SHU	main, master	grapheme	4f1.1, 1938, 285

I18	注	soso(gu), CHŪ	pour, concentration	water, master	3a5.16, 325, 2531
I18	柱	hashira, CHŪ	pillar	wood, master	4a5.12, 896, 2236
I18	駐	CHŪ	resident	horse, master	10a5.2, 1826, 5209
I18	住	su(mu), JŪ	live, reside	human being, master	2a5.19, 64, 404
I18	往	Ō	coming and going	step, master	3i5.6, 292, 1605
I19	差	sa(su), SA	pour, difference	lamb's wool, drop, handicraft	2o8.4, 3311, 3662
I19	着	tsu(ku/keru), ki(ru/seru), CHAKU	arrive, put on	lamb's wool, drop, eye	2o10.1, 3316, 3665
I19	養	yashina(u), YŌ	foster, support	lamb's wool, drop, drop, good	2o13.1, 2365, 3671
I19	美	utsuku(shii), BI	beautiful	lamb's wool, big	2o7.4, 2264, 3658
I19	善	yo(i), ZEN	good, *better*	lamb's wool, horns, mouth	2o10.2, 2325, 606
I19	繕	tsukuro(u), ZEN	mend	thread, better	6a12.2, 1423, 3612

J1	木	ki, BOKU, MOKU	tree	grapheme	4a0.1, 3450, 2170
J1	朴	BOKU	simple, plain	wood, divining rod	4a2.3, 819, 2176
J1	森	mori, SHIN	forest	tree, tree, tree	4a8.39, 2475, 2301
J1	休	yasu(mu/meru), KYŪ	rest, give a rest	human being, tree	2a4.2, 52, 380
J1	床	toko, yuka, SHŌ	bed, floor	building, wood	3q4.1, 3067, 1503
J1	枚	MAI	counter for flat things	wood, teacher	4a4.4, 859, 2202
J1	杉	sugi	Japanese cedar	tree, style	4a3.2, 832, 2190
J1	保	tamo(tsu), HO	*preserve*	human being, mouth, tree	2a7.11, 96, 455
J1	困	koma(ru), KON	be in trouble, be distressed	enclosed, tree	3s4.1, 3070, 1033
J1	閑	KAN	leisure	gate, tree	8e4.2, 3322, 4948
J2	菜	na, SAI	vegetable	flower, harvest	3k8.25, 2305, 3982

J2	採	to(ru), SAI	pick, gather	hand, harvest	3c8.14, 499, 1947
J2	彩	irodo(ru), SAI	color	harvest, style	3j8.1, 1681, 1590
J3	操	ayatsu(ru), SŌ	manipulate	hand, bird's nest	3c13.3, 769, 2015
J3	燥	SŌ	dry up	fire, bird's nest	4d13.6, 1087, 2810
J3	藻	mo, SŌ	algae	flower, water, bird's nest	3k16.8, 2384, 4098
J3	繰	ku(ru)	reel, wind	thread, bird's nest	6a13.3, 1427, 3619
J4	林	hayashi, RIN	forest	grapheme	4a4.1, 861, 2210
J4	禁	KIN	*prohibition*	forest, show	4e8.3, 2795, 3251
J4	襟	eri, KIN	collar	robe, prohibition	5e13.2, 1252, 4267
J4	暦	koyomi, REKI	calendar	cliff, forest, sun	2p12.3, 3018, 833
J5	麻	asa, MA	hemp	grapheme	3q8.3, 3125, 5390

J5	磨	miga(ku), MA	polish	hemp, stone	3g13.3, 3181, 5393
J5	摩	MA	rub	hemp, hand	3g12.6, 3175, 5392
J6	本	moto, HON	basis, book, counter for cylindrical objects	grapheme	0a5.25, 3502, 96
J6	体	karada, TAI	body, form	human being, basis	2a5.6, 71, 405
J6	鉢	HACHI	bowl	metal, basis	8a5.4, 1708, 4840
J7	未	MI	not yet	grapheme	0a5.27, 3506, 179
J7	味	aji(wau), aji, MI	taste, savor	mouth, not yet	3d5.3, 274, 913
J7	妹	imōto, MAI	younger sister	woman, not yet	3e5.4, 278, 1204
J7	業	waza, GYŌ, GŌ	deed, business	(line up), horns, not yet	0a13.3, 2612, 143
J8	末	sue, MATSU, BATSU	last part	grapheme	0a5.26, 3505, 177
J8	抹	MATSU	wipe out, pulverize	hand, last part	3c5.9, 313, 1870

J9	述	no(beru), JUTSU	state	resin, traveler	2g5.3, 3075, 4675
J9	術	JUTSU	technique	resin, (go)	3i8.2, 476, 1621
J10	米	kome, BEI, MAI	rice, America	grapheme	6b0.1, 3529, 3461
J10	来	ku(ru), kita(ru), RAI	come	one, rice	0a7.6, 3551, 202
J10	迷	mayo(u), MEI	be perplexed, be in doubt	rice, traveler	2q6.1, 3092, 4681
J10	楼	RŌ	tower	tree, rice, woman	4a9.10, 1019, 2322
J10	類	RUI	kind, type	rice, big, head	9a9.1, 1807, 5138
J10	数	kazo(eru), kazu, SŪ	count, number	rice, woman, teacher	4i9.1, 1790, 2057
J11	束	taba, SOKU	bundle	grapheme	0a7.8, 3554, 196
J11	速	haya(i), sumi(yaka), SOKU	quick, prompt	bundle, traveler	2q7.4, 3105, 4700
J11	勅	CHOKU	imperial decree	bundle, power	2g7.1, 1451, 725

J11	頼	tano(mu), tayo(ru), RAI	ask, *rely on*	bundle, head	9a7.1, 1615, 5129
J11	瀬	se	shallow, rapids	water, rely on	3a16.3, 806, 2735
J12	東	higashi, TŌ	east	grapheme	0a8.9, 3568, 213
J12	凍	kō(ru), kogo(eru), TŌ	freeze	ice, east	2b8.2, 129, 649
J12	棟	mune, TŌ	*ridge of a roof*	wood, east	4a8.3, 991, 2299
J12	陳	CHIN	set forth, explain	fortress, east	2d8.2, 540, 5001
J12	練	ne(ru), REN	knead, training	thread, east	6a8.2, 1375, 3565
J12	錬	REN	temper, harden	metal, east	8a8.3, 1741, 4881
J12	欄	RAN	column	(ridge of a roof), gate	4a16.4, 1110, 2401
K1	奔	HON	rush	big, nosegay	2k6.5, 2218, 1175
K1	暁	akatsuki, GYŌ	dawn	sun, nosegay, one, legs	4c8.1, 980, 2139

K1	焼	ya(keru/ku), SHŌ	burn, roast	fire, nosegay, one, legs	4d8.4, 997, 2772
K1	噴	fu(ku), FUN	spout	mouth, nosegay, money	3d12.8, 717, 995
K1	憤	ikidō(ru), FUN	be angry	feeling, nosegay, money	4k12.6, 730, 1773
K1	墳	FUN	burial mound	earth, nosegay, money	3b12.1, 719, 1141
K2	研	to(gu), KEN	sharpen, research	stone, with both hands	5a4.1, 1132, 3180
K2	開	hira(ku), KAI	open	gate, with both hands	8e4.6, 3321, 4950
K2	形	katachi, kata, KEI, GYŌ	shape	with both hands, style	3j4.1, 846, 1589
K2	刑	KEI	*penalty*	with both hands, sword	2f4.2, 830, 670
K2	型	kata, KEI	type	penalty, earth	3b6.11, 2638, 1077
K2	併	awa(seru), HEI	join together	human being, (horns), with both hands	2a6.17, 83, 425
K3	寛	KAN	tolerant	house, flexible, see	3m10.3, 2327, 1325

K3	鼻	hana, BI	nose	nose, rice field, flexible	5f9.3, 2706, 5421
K3	算	SAN	calculate	bamboo, eye, flexible	6f8.7, 2702, 3415
K4	庶	SHO	*manifold*	building, leather, cooking fire	3q8.7, 3127, 1522
K4	遮	saegi(ru), SHA	interrupt	manifold, traveler	2q11.4, 3158, 4737
K4	席	SEKI	seat	building, leather, cloth	3q7.4, 3113, 1513
K5	革	kawa, KAKU	leather, reform	grapheme	3k6.2, 2448, 5088
K5	覇	HA	supremacy	west, reform, moon	4b15.4, 2730, 4281
K6	甘	ama(eru/yakasu), ama(i), KAN	pamper, sweet	grapheme	0a5.32, 3494, 2988
K6	紺	KON	dark blue	thread, sweet	6a5.5, 1332, 3517
K7	某	BŌ	a certain	grapheme	4a5.33, 2560, 2989
K7	謀	haka(ru), BŌ	scheme, conspire	words, a certain	7a9.8, 1593, 4414

K7	媒	BAI	intermediate	woman, a certain	3e9.2, 564, 1241
K8	棋	KI	Japanese chess	wood, game	4a8.14, 987, 2294
K8	期	KI	term, period	game, moon	4b8.11, 1704, 3785
K8	基	moto, KI	base	game, earth	3b8.12, 2673, 1098
K8	碁	GO	Japanese checkers	game, stone	5a8.9, 2699, 3202
K9	井	i, SEI	well	grapheme	0a4.46, 3454, 165
K9	囲	kako(mu), I	enclose	enclosed, well	3s4.2, 3069, 1032
K9	耕	tagaya(su), KŌ	plow, cultivate	two, tree, well	0a10.13, 1308, 3695
K10	黄	ki, KŌ, Ō	*yellow*	herbs, reason, animal legs	3k8.16, 2468, 5399
K10	横	yoko, Ō	side, flank	tree, yellow	4a11.13, 1066, 2361
K10	散	chi(ru/rasu), SAN	scatter (vi, vt)	herbs, part of the body, teacher	4i8.1, 1702, 2056

K11	昔	mukashi, SEKI	former times	grapheme	3k5.28, 2432, 2108
K11	惜	o(shimu), SEKI	regret	feeling, former times	4k8.11, 484, 1712
K11	籍	SEKI	register	bamboo, two, tree, former times	6f14.1, 2731, 3450
K11	錯	SAKU	mixed up	metal, former times	8a8.10, 1743, 4880
K11	借	ka(riru), SHAKU	borrow	human being, former times	2a8.22, 122, 490
K11	措	SO	measure, step	hand, former times	3c8.20, 502, 1930
K12	共	tomo, KYŌ	joint	grapheme	3k3.3, 2393, 581
K12	供	sona(eru), tomo, KYŌ	sacrifice attendant	human being, joint	2a6.13, 88, 431
K12	恭	uyauya(shii), KYŌ	respectful	joint, (heart)	3k7.16, 2459, 1680
K12	洪	KŌ	flood	water, joint	3a6.14, 386, 2544
K12	異	koto, I	*different*	rice field, joint	5f6.7, 2584, 3008

K12	翼	tsubasa, YOKU	wing	feather, different	2o15.2, 2720, 3680
L1	畳	tata(mi), JŌ	tatami, fold up	rice field, cover, additionally	5f7.3, 2592, 3010
L1	帯	o(biru), TAI	wear, *belt*	one, mountain, cover, cloth	3f7.1, 2582, 1474
L1	滞	todokō(ru), TAI	stagnate, stay	water, belt	3a10.14, 663, 2661
L1	策	SAKU	scheme, measure	bamboo, (tree), cloth	6f6.2, 2679, 3393
L1	刺	sa(saru/su), SHI	pierce, be stuck	(tree), cloth, sword	2f6.2, 1275, 682
L2	栄	saka(eru), EI	flourish, glory	school house, tree	3n6.1, 2574, 2239
L2	労	RŌ	labor	school house, power	3n4.3, 2548, 720
L2	覚	sa(meru/masu), obo(eru), KAKU	awake (vi), wake up (vt), remember	school house, see	3n9.3, 3604, 4288
L2	学	mana(bu), GAKU	study, school	school house, child	3n4.2, 2555, 1271
L2	営	itona(mu), EI	manage	school house, management	3n9.2, 2603, 963

L2	蛍	hotaru, KEI	firefly	school house, insect	3n8.2, 2591, 4176
L3	常	tsune, JŌ	normal, regular	elite, cloth	3n8.3, 2590, 1364
L3	党	TŌ	party	elite, legs	3n7.2, 2581, 1363
L3	堂	DŌ	hall	elite, earth	3n8.4, 2589, 1365
L3	賞	SHŌ	*prize*	elite, money	3n12.1, 2618, 1372
L3	償	tsuguna(u), SHŌ	compensate	human being, prize	2a15.4, 176, 563
L3	掌	SHŌ	take charge of, palm	elite, hand	3n9.4, 2602, 1366
L4	売	u(ru), BAI	sell	grapheme	3p4.3, 2196, 1067
L4	読	yo(mu), DOKU	read	words, sell	7a7.9, 1541, 4375
L4	続	tsuzu(ku/keru), ZOKU	continue (vi, vt)	thread, sell	6a7.5, 1362, 3544
L5	軍	GUN	army	grapheme	2i7.1, 2080, 628

L5	輝	kagaya(ku), KI	glitter, shine	light, army	7c8.8, 1402, 1371
L5	揮	KI	shake, wield	hand, army	3c9.14, 589, 1960
L5	運	hako(bu), UN	transport	army, traveler	2q9.10, 3140, 4725
L6	南	minami, NAN	*south*	ten, cavity, horns, ten	2k7.1, 2082, 778
L6	奥	oku, Ō	inner part	drop, cavity, rice, big	6b6.9, 2824, 240
L6	向	mu(ku/keru), mu(kō), KŌ	face, turn toward, the other side	drop, cavity, mouth	3d3.10, 3052, 101
L6	尚	SHŌ	value	small, cavity, mouth	3n5.2, 2233, 1361
L6	雨	ame, ama, U	rain	one, cavity, halve, drop, drop, drop, drop	8d0.1, 3561, 5042
L6	両	RYŌ	*both*	one, cavity, mountain	0a6.11, 3518, 34
L6	満	mi(chiru/tasu), MAN	be filled, fill	water, flower, both	3a9.25, 607, 2636
L7	内	uchi, NAI	inside	grapheme	0a4.23, 3466, 82

L7	納	osa(maru/meru), NŌ	be paid, obtain	thread, inside	6a4.5, 1300, 3508
L7	丙	HEI	*third class*	one, inside	0a5.21, 3479, 22
L7	柄	gara, HEI	character, handle	wood, third class	4a5.9, 987, 2234
L7	病	ya(mu), yamai, BYŌ, HEI	fall ill, illness	sickness, third class	5i5.3, 3277, 3042
L7	肉	NIKU	*flesh*	inside, human being	2a4.20, 3200, 3724
L7	腐	kusa(ru/rasu), FU	rot (vi, vt)	urban prefecture, flesh	3q11.3, 3162, 1532
L8	同	ona(ji), DŌ	same	grapheme	2r4.2, 2987, 619
L8	洞	hora, DŌ	cave	water, same	3a6.25, 380, 2546
L8	銅	DŌ	copper	metal, same	8a6.12, 1721, 4853
L8	胴	DŌ	trunk	part of the body, same	4b6.10, 950, 3767
L8	筒	tsutsu, TŌ	tube	bamboo, same	6f6.15, 2680, 3392

L9	周	mawa(ri), SHŪ	periphery	grapheme	2r6.1, 2998, 622
L9	週	SHŪ	week	periphery, traveler	2q8.7, 3122, 4707
L9	調	shira(beru), CHŌ	investigate, prepare, tone	words, periphery	7a8.16, 1567, 4392
L9	彫	ho(ru), CHŌ	carve	periphery, style	3j8.2, 1683, 236
L10	渦	uzu, KA	whirlpool, vortex	water, danger	3a9.36, 603, 2629
L10	禍	KA	calamity	altar, danger	4e9.4, 1030, 3254
L10	過	su(giru), KA	exceed	danger, traveler	2q9.18, 3137, 4723
L10	骨	hone, KOTSU	*bone*	(danger), part of the body	4b6.14, 2654, 5236
L10	滑	sube(ru), name(raka),KATSU	slide	water, bone	3a10.6, 658, 2663
L11	鋼	hagane, KŌ	steel	metal, steel	8a8.20, 1740, 4883
L11	綱	tsuna, KŌ	rope	thread, steel	6a8.23, 1372, 3561

L11	剛	GŌ	tough	steel, sword	2f8.7, 1673, 114
L12	耐	ta(eru), TAI	endure, withstand	beard, a bit of	2r7.1, 1282, 3690
L12	需	JU	*demand*	rain, beard	8d6.1, 2797, 5052
L12	儒	JU	Confucianism	human being, demand	2a14.1, 174, 561
L13	偶	GŪ	by chance	human being, scorpion	2a9.1, 132, 508
L13	隅	sumi, GŪ	nook	fortress, scorpion	2d9.1, 623, 5009
L13	遇	GŪ	encounter	scorpion, traveler	2q9.1, 3135, 4715
L13	愚	oro(ka), GU	foolishness	scorpion, heart	4k9.15, 2834, 1730
L14	月	tsuki, GETSU, GATSU	moon, month	grapheme	4b0.1, 2956, 2169
L14	前	mae, ZEN	before	horns, part of the body, sword	2o7.3, 2266, 595
L14	明	aka(rui), aki(raka), MEI, MYŌ	bright, clear	sun, moon	4c4.1, 855, 2110

L14	盟	MEI	alliance	sun, moon, plate	5h8.1, 2794, 3119
L14	崩	kuzu(reru/su), HŌ	crumble (vi), destroy (vt)	mountain, moon, moon	3o8.7, 2296, 1430
L14	棚	tana	shelf	wood, moon, moon	4a8.10, 984, 2300
L15	肖	SHŌ	resemblance	grapheme	3n4.1, 2205, 1360
L15	消	ki(eru)/ke(su), SHŌ	extinguish	water, resemble	3a7.16, 443, 2574
L15	硝	SHŌ	saltpeter	stone, resemble	5a7.6, 1185, 3192
L15	宵	yoi, SHŌ	early evening	house, resemble	3m7.7, 2276, 1307
L15	削	kezu(ru), SAKU	chip, splinter	resemble, sword	2f7.4, 1448, 690
L16	用	mochi(iru), YŌ	use, adopt business, work	grapheme	2r3.1, 2976, 2993
L16	備	sona(waru/eru), BI	be furnished with, furnish	human being, flower, cliff, use	2a10.4, 146, 519
L16	踊	odo(ru), YŌ	dance	foot, typical, use	7d7.2, 1558, 4565

L16	通	tō(ru/su), kayo(u), TSŪ	pass, let pass, commute	typical, use, traveler	2q7.18, 3109, 4703
L16	痛	ita(mu/meru), ita(i), TSŪ	feel pain (vi), inflict, pain (vt)	sickness, typical, use	5i7.7, 3285, 3054
L17	浦	ura, HO	seashore, bay	water, fishing rod	3a7.2, 437, 2571
L17	捕	tsuka(maru/maeru), to(ru), HO	be caught (vi), catch (vt)	hand, fishing rod	3c7.3, 429, 1919
L17	補	ogina(u), HO	supplement	robe, fishing rod	5e7.1, 1194, 4242
L18	円	EN	circle, yen	grapheme	2r2.1, 2955, 617
L18	角	kado, tsuno, KAKU	*angle*, horn	tied up, circle, one	2n5.1, 2047, 4301
L18	触	sawa(ru), fu(reru), SHOKU	touch	angle, insect	6d7.10, 1518, 4305
L18	解	to(ku), KAI	dissolve	angle, sword, cattle	4g9.1, 1517, 4306
L19	冊	SATSU, SAKU	counter for books	grapheme	0a5.42, 3483, 88
L20	再	futata(bi), SAI	another time, again	grapheme	0a6.26, 3519, 35

L21	溝	mizo, KŌ	ditch, gutter	water, structure	3a10.9, 659, 2657
L21	構	kama(eru), KŌ	construct	wood, structure	4a10.10, 1049, 2343
L21	講	KŌ	lecture	words, structure	7a10.3, 1619, 4425
L21	購	KŌ	purchase	money, structure	7b10.3, 1624, 4522
L22	舟	fune, SHŪ	ship	grapheme	6c0.1, 3538, 3863
L22	舶	HAKU	ship	ship, white	6c5.2, 1340, 3870
L22	艇	TEI	boat	ship, court	6c6.2, 1365, 3875
L22	丹	TAN	red, pills	ship	0a4.34, 3441, 163
L23	机	tsukue, KI	desk	wood, table	4a2.4, 820, 2174
L23	飢	u(eru), KI	starve	eat, table	8b2.1, 1668, 5155
L23	肌	hada	skin	part of the body, table	4b2.2, 827, 3726

L23	冗	JŌ	redundant	cover, table	2i2.2, 1976, 625
L23	風	kaze, FŪ	*wind*	table, drop, insect	2s7.1, 3007, 5148
L23	猟	RYŌ	hunting	watchdog, gather, table, two, halve	3g8.6, 538, 2894
L24	凡	BON, HAN	common, ordinary	grapheme	2s1.1, 2938, 654
L24	帆	ho, HAN	sail	cloth, common	3f3.1, 210, 1469
L24	恐	oso(reru), KYŌ	fear	handicraft, common, heart	4k6.19, 1650, 1685
L24	築	kizu(ku), CHIKU	construct	bamboo, handicraft, common, wood	6f10.5, 2715, 3435
M1	六	mut(tsu), ROKU	six	cap, animal legs	2j2.2, 1965, 283
M1	卒	SOTSU	graduate	cap, human being, human being, ten	2j6.2, 2055, 294
M1	壇	DAN	platform	earth, cap, turn around, sunrise	3b13.5, 754, 1146
M1	坑	KŌ	pit	earth, cap, table	3b4.6, 236, 1063

M1	抗	KŌ	resist	hand, cap, table	3c4.15, 252, 1852
M1	航	KŌ	navigate	ship, cap, table	6c4.2, 1318, 3867
M2	高	taka(i), KŌ	*high*	watchtower, cavity, mouth	2j8.6, 2097, 5248
M2	稿	KŌ	manuscript	rice seedling, high	5d10.5, 1231, 3299
M2	享	KYŌ	*enjoy*	watchtower, child	2j5.1, 2037, 293
M2	郭	KAKU	red-light district	enjoy, city wall	2d7.14, 1678, 4765
M2	亭	TEI	*Japanese restaurant*	watchtower, cover, block of houses	2j7.5, 2072, 303
M2	停	TEI	halt	human being, Japanese restaurant	2a9.14, 139, 507
M3	京	KYŌ, KEI	capital, governmental seat	grapheme	2j6.3, 2052, 295
M3	涼	suzu(mu), suzu(shii), RYŌ	refresh, cool	water, capital	3a8.31, 521, 2598
M3	鯨	kujira, GEI	whale	fish, capital	11a8.9, 1882, 5307

M3	景	KEI	*scene*, view	sun, capital	4c8.8, 2470, 2142
M3	影	kage, EI	shadow	scene, style	3j12.1, 1889, 1594
M4	市	ichi, SHI	city, market	grapheme	2j3.1, 1993, 284
M4	姉	ane, SHI	older sister	woman, market	3e5.8, 280, 1207
M4	肺	HAI	lung	part of the body, market	4b5.9, 916, 3752
M5	亡	na(i), BŌ	deceased	grapheme	2j1.1, 3402, 281
M5	忙	isoga(shii), BŌ	busy	feeling, deceased	4k3.2, 214, 1647
M5	忘	wasu(reru), BŌ	forget	deceased, heart	2j5.4, 2036, 291
M5	望	nozo(mu), BŌ, MŌ	hope, wish	deceased, moon, king	4f7.6, 2742, 2940
M5	妄	MŌ, BŌ	delusion	deceased, woman	2j4.6, 2016, 288
M5	盲	mekura, MŌ	blind	deceased, eye	2j6.6, 2053, 297

M5	網	ami, MŌ	net	thread, cavity, horns, deceased	6a8.25, 1374, 3563
M5	荒	a(reru/rasu), ara(i), KŌ	devastate, *be wild*	flower, deceased, river	3k6.18, 2260, 3941
M5	慌	awa(teru), KŌ	be in a flurry	feeling, be wild	4k9.10, 580, 1725
M6	方	kata, HŌ	way of doing, person, direction	grapheme	4h0.1, 1963, 2082
M6	芳	kanba(shii), HŌ	fragrant	flower, direction	3k4.1, 2210, 3907
M6	放	hana(tsu), hana(reru/su), HŌ	*let go* (vt), free oneself	direction, teacher	4h4.1, 853, 2084
M6	倣	nara(u), HŌ	imitate	human being, let go	2a8.7, 113, 466
M6	訪	tazu(neru), otozu(reru), HŌ	visit	words, direction	7a4.1, 1468, 4326
M6	坊	BŌ	priest's residence	earth, direction	3b4.1, 233, 1062
M6	防	fuse(gu), BŌ	prevent	fortress, direction	2d4.1, 270, 4980
M6	肪	BŌ	fat	part of the body, direction	4b4.2, 877, 3734

M6	妨	samata(geru), BŌ	hinder	woman, direction	3e4.1, 238, 1196
M6	紡	tsumu(gu), BŌ	spin	thread, direction	6a4.1, 1295, 3505
M6	旗	hata, KI	flag	direction, human, game	4h10.1, 1047, 2093
M6	族	ZOKU	family	direction, human, arrow	4h7.3, 958, 2090
M6	遊	aso(bu), YŪ, YU	play, amuse oneself	direction, human, child, traveler	2q8.3, 3142, 4726
M6	敷	shi(ku), FU	spread, lay	alms, drop, direction, teacher	4i11.1, 1870, 2059
M6	激	hage(shii), GEKI	violent	water, white, direction, teacher	3a13.1, 776, 2712
M7	文	fumi, BUN, MON	letter, writings	grapheme	2j2.4, 1962, 2064
M7	対	TAI, TSUI	opposite, oppose, pair	writings, a bit of	2j5.5, 831, 2067
M7	紋	MON	crest	thread, writings	6a4.9, 1299, 3507
M7	蚊	ka	mosquito	insect, writings	6a4.5, 1319, 4123

M8	斉	SEI	uniform, equal	grapheme	2j6.5, 2054, 5423
M8	剤	ZAI	mixture, medicine	equal, sword	2f8.6, 1669, 5424
M8	済	su(mu/masu), SAI	settle, finish	water, equal	3a8.30, 522, 2597
M8	斎	SAI	study room	equal, small	2j9.6, 2115, 5425
M9	交	ma(jiru/zeru), ka(u/wasu), KŌ	intermingle (vi), mix (vt), intercourse	grapheme	2j4.3, 2015, 290
M9	効	ki(ku), KŌ	work, be effective	intermingle, power	2g6.2, 1265, 722
M9	郊	KŌ	suburb	intermingle, city wall	2d6.8, 1286, 4761
M9	校	KŌ	school	tree, intermingle	4a6.24, 929, 2260
M9	絞	shi(maru/meru), shibo(ru), KŌ	strangled, wring	thread, intermingle	6a6.9, 1349, 3535
M9	較	KAKU	comparison	vehicle, intermingle	7c6.3, 1536, 4623
M10	恋	ko(u), koi(shii), REN	love, beloved	pink, heart	2j8.2, 2098, 313

M10	蛮	BAN	barbarian	pink, insect	2j10.1, 2129, 322
M10	跡	ato, SEKI	trace	foot, pink	7d6.7, 1534, 4560
M11	立	ta(tsu/teru), RITSU, RYŪ	stand, establish	grapheme	5b0.1, 1992, 3343
M11	位	kurai, I	rank, position	human being, stand	2a5.1, 61, 401
M11	泣	na(ku), KYŪ	cry	water, stand	3a5.1, 338, 2532
M11	粒	tsubu, RYŪ	grain	rice, stand	6b5.1, 1328, 3471
M11	翌	YOKU	the following	feather, stand	5b6.6, 2668, 3674
M11	端	hashi, hata, TAN	edge	stand, mountain, beard	5b9.2, 1221, 3363
M11	接	tsu(gu), SETSU	piece together, contact	hand, stand, woman	3c8.10, 500, 1951
M11	童	warabe, DŌ	*little child*	stand, countryside	5b7.3, 2130, 3357
M11	鐘	kane, SHŌ	bell	metal, little child	8a12.6, 1769, 4917

M12	培	tsuchika(u), BAI	cultivate, foster	earth, group of people	3b8.6, 464, 1091
M12	陪	BAI	accompany	fortress, group of people	2d8.3, 539, 5002
M12	倍	BAI	double, times	human being, group of people	2a8.14, 108, 483
M12	賠	BAI	compensation	money, group of people	7b8.1, 1582, 4512
M12	部	BU	section	group of people, city wall	2d8.15, 1676, 4767
M12	剖	BŌ	dissect	group of people, sword	2f8.1, 1670, 693
M12	競	kiso(u), se(ru), KYŌ, KEI	compete	stand, (older brother), stand, older brother	5b15.1, 1566, 3364
M13	音	oto, ne, ON	sound	grapheme	5b4.3, 2070, 5110
M13	暗	kura(i), AN	dark	sun, sound	4c9.2, 1010, 2154
M13	韻	IN	rhyme	sound, member	7b12.2, 1811, 5115
M13	境	sakai, KYŌ	boundary, region	earth, sound, legs	3b11.1, 676, 1135

M13	鏡	kagami, KYŌ	mirror	metal, sound legs	8a11.6, 1766, 4912
M14	章	SHŌ	chapter, badge	grapheme	5b6.3, 2117, 5112
M14	彰	SHŌ	proclamation	chapter, style	3j11.1, 1860, 1593
M14	障	sawa(ru), SHŌ	hinder, harm	fortress, chapter	2d11.2, 715, 5019
M15	意	I	will	grapheme	5b8.2, 2136, 5113
M15	億	OKU	hundred million	human being, will	2a13.6, 170, 551
M15	憶	OKU	remember	feeling, will	4k13.5, 765, 1780
M16	新	atara(shii), ara(ta), SHIN	new	first time, ax	5b8.3, 1784, 2080
M16	薪	takigi, SHIN	firewood	flower, first time, ax	3k13.3, 2374, 4069
M16	親	shita(shii), oya, SHIN	intimate, parent	first time, see	5b11.1, 1799, 4293
M17	辛	kara(i), SHIN	hot, pungent	grapheme	5b2.2, 2038, 4646

M17	辞	ya(meru), JI	resign, speech	tongue, hot	5b8.4, 1364, 3860
M17	宰	SAI	rule, preside over	house, hot	3m7.2, 2275, 1303
M18	帝	TEI	emperor	emperor, cloth	2j7.1, 2073, 305
M18	締	shi(maru/meru), TEI	tighten (vi, vt), conclude (a treaty)	thread, emperor, cloth	6a9.11, 1393, 3581
M18	傍	katawa(ra), BŌ	beside	human being, emperor, direction	2a10.6, 147, 520
M19	商	akina(u), SHŌ	trade	counsel, legs, mouth	2j9.7, 2116, 321
M19	滴	shitata(ru), shizuku, TEKI	drop	water, counsel, old	3a11.14, 705, 2674
M19	適	TEKI	suitable	counsel, old, traveler	2q11.3, 3167, 4738
M19	摘	tsu(mu), TEKI	pick	hand, counsel, old	3c11.5, 694, 1987
M19	敵	kataki, TEKI	enemy	counsel, old, teacher	4i11.2, 1864, 2060
M19	嫡	CHAKU	legitimate	woman, counsel, old	3e11.5, 680, 1253

M20	産	u(mareru/mu), SAN	be born (vi), give birth (vt), produce	stamina, life	5b6.4, 3298, 3354
M20	顔	kao, GAN	face	stamina, style, head	9a9.3, 1808, 5139
N1	札	fuda, SATSU	paper money, bill	wood, hook	4a1.1, 817, 2171
N1	礼	REI, RAI	etiquette, rite	altar, hook	4e1.1, 818, 3229
N1	孔	KŌ	*open hole*	child, hook	2c1.1, 179, 1265
N1	乳	chichi, chi, NYŪ	milk	caress, open hole	3n4.4, 1438, 266
N1	乱	mida(reru/su), RAN	be disordered, put into disorder	tongue, hook	3d4.21, 1260, 3856
N2	乙	OTSU	second class	grapheme	0a1.5, 3339, 260
N2	乾	kawa(ku/kasu), KAN	dry (vi, vt)	fog, human, second class	4c7.14, 1679, 784
N2	迅	JIN	swift	second class, ten, traveler	2q3.5, 3046, 4664
N2	飛	to(bu/basu), HI	fly	second class, drop, drop, bottle, second class, drop,drop	0a9.4, 3572, 5152

N2	気	KI, KE	spirit, soul, air	human, one, second class, scissors	0a6.8, 3194, 2480
N2	汽	KI	steam	water, human, one, second class	3a4.16, 264, 2507
N3	心	kokoro, SHIN	heart	grapheme	4k0.1, 11, 1645
N3	応	Ō	respond	building, heart	3q4.2, 3066, 1504
N3	悠	YŪ	leisure	human being, halve, teacher, heart	4k7.20, 2741, 1701
N4	必	kanara(zu), HITSU	without fail	grapheme	0a5.16, 15, 129
N4	泌	HITSU, HI	secrete	water, without fail	3a5.10, 332, 2522
N4	秘	hi(meru), HI	keep secret	rice seedling, without fail	5d5.6, 1159, 3281
N4	密	MITSU	close, secret	house, without fail, mountain	3m8.5, 2292, 1316
N5	突	tsu(ku), TOTSU	thrust protruding	airhole, big	3m5.11, 2230, 3316
N5	空	a(ku/keru), kara, sora, KŪ	become vacant, *empty*, sky, air	airhole, handicraft	3m5.12, 2227, 3317

N5	控	hika(eru), KŌ	hold back, wait	hand, empty	3c8.11, 495, 1941
N5	搾	shibo(ru), SAKU	squeeze	hand, airhole, generate	3c10.9, 649, 1975
N5	窯	kama, YŌ	kiln	airhole, lamb's wool, cooking fire	3m12.5, 2361, 3336
N5	深	fuka(i), SHIN	deep	water, cover, legs, wood	3a8.21, 524, 2606
N5	探	saga(su), TAN	probe, search	hand, cover, legs, wood	3c8.16, 505, 1949
N6	元	moto, GEN, GAN	origin	grapheme	0a4.5, 1929, 275
N6	頑	GAN	stubborn	origin, head	9a4.6, 1040, 5122
N6	完	KAN	*completion*	house, origin	3m4.6, 2201, 1288
N6	冠	kanmuri, KAN	crown	cover, origin, a bit of	2i7.2, 2081, 627
N6	院	IN	institution	fortress, completion	2d7.9, 454, 4991
N6	微	BI	slight	step, mountain, one, (legs), teacher	3i10.1, 639, 1631

N7	西	nishi, SEI, SAI	west	grapheme	0a6.20, 3520, 4273
N7	酒	sake, SHU	alcoholic drink, sake	water, wine	3a7.1, 444, 2573
N7	猶	YŪ	delay	watchdog, drop, drop, wine	3g9.5, 619, 2897
N7	尊	tōto(bu), tatto(i), SON	*honor*	drop, drop, wine, a bit of	2o10.3, 2324, 607
N7	遵	JUN	obey	honor, traveler	2q12.8, 3167, 4742
N8	沈	shizu(mu/meru), CHIN	sink	water, (sink)	3a4.9, 261, 2508
N8	就	tsu(ku/keru), SHŪ	settle in	capital, sink, drop	3d9.21, 1694, 323
N8	既	sude(ni), KI	*already*	(solid), one, drop, sink	0a10.5, 1166, 3887
N8	慨	GAI	deplore	feeling, already	4k10.3, 641, 1741
N8	概	GAI	general, approximate	tree, already	4a10.2, 1048, 2344
N9	老	o(iru), fu(keru), RŌ	grow old, old	earth, drop, crouch	2k4.5, 3197, 3683

N9	蛇	hebi, JA, DA	snake	insect, house, crouch	6d5.7, 1343, 4130
N9	壱	ICHI	one	scholar, cover, crouch	3p4.2, 2197, 1059
N10	化	ba(keru/kasu), KA, KE	change into	grapheme	2a2.6, 21, 350
N10	花	hana, KA	flower	flower, change into	3k4.7, 2211, 3909
N10	貨	KA	money, goods	change into, money	7b4.5, 2465, 4493
N10	靴	kutsu, KA	shoes	reform, change into	3k10.34, 1781, 5092
N10	傾	katamu(ku/keru), KEI	incline (vi, vt)	change into, head	2a11.3, 154, 534
N11	比	kura(beru), HI	compare	grapheme	2m3.5, 26, 2470
N11	批	HI	critique	hand, compare	3c4.13, 250, 1848
N11	皆	mina, KAI	*all*	compare, white	4c5.14, 2445, 2471
N11	階	KAI	floor, rank	fortress, all	2d9.6, 624, 5011

N11	陛	HEI	steps to the imperial palace	fortress, compare, earth	2d7.6, 453, 4988
N11	昆	KON	insect, *descendants*	sun, compare	4c4.10, 2413, 2106
N11	混	ma(zaru/zeru), KON	blend, mix	water, descendants	3a8.14, 519, 2604
N12	北	kita, HOKU	north	grapheme	0a5.5, 197, 751
N12	背	somu(ku/keru), se, HAI	contrary to (vi), avert (vt), back	north, part of the body	4b5.15, 2573, 3754
N13	旨	mune, SHI	purport	grapheme	4c2.2, 2024, 752
N13	指	sa(su), yubi, SHI	point, finger	hand, purport	3c6.15, 378, 1904
N13	脂	abura, SHI	oil	part of the body, purport	4b6.7, 954, 3766
N14	兆	kiza(su), kiza(shi), CHŌ	omen, trillion	grapheme	2b4.4, 225, 637
N14	挑	ido(mu), CHŌ	provoke	hand, trillion	3c6.5, 372, 1898
N14	眺	naga(meru), CHŌ	look at, gaze at	eye, trillion	5c6.2, 1171, 3138

N14	跳	to(bu), ha(neru), CHŌ	jump	foot, trillion	7d6.3, 1532, 4562
N14	桃	momo, TŌ	peach	tree, trillion	4a6.10, 936, 2255
N14	逃	ni(geru/gasu), TŌ	escape (vi), let go (vt)	trillion, traveler	2q6.5, 3095, 4682
N15	七	nana, nana(tsu), SHICHI	seven	grapheme	0a2.13, 3362, 261
N15	切	ki(reru/ru), SETSU	*cut*	seven, sword	2f2.2, 27, 667
N15	窃	SETSU	steal	airhole, cut	3m6.5, 2253, 3320
N15	宅	TAKU	home, house	house, drop, seven	3m3.4, 2174, 1279
N15	託	TAKU	request, entrust	words, drop, seven	7a3.1, 1455, 4315
N16	慮	RYO	thought, concern	tiger, think	2m13.2, 3266, 4112
N16	虜	RYO	captive	tiger, man	2m11.2, 3255, 4111
N16	膚	FU	skin	tiger, stomach	2m13.1, 3265, 4113

N16	虚	KYO	void, useless	tiger, (line up)	2m9.1, 3237, 4109
N17	毛	ke, MŌ	hair	grapheme	0a4.33, 3453, 2473
N17	耗	MŌ	wear out, decrease	two, tree, hair	0a10.12, 1309, 3694
N18	屯	TON	barracks	grapheme	0a4.35, 3457, 264
N18	鈍	nibu(ru), nibu(i), DON	dull	metal, barracks	8a4.2, 1689, 4830
N18	純	JUN	pure	thread, barracks	6a4.3, 1297, 3509
N19	竜	tatsu, RYŪ	*dragon*	stand, lightning	5b5.3, 2099, 5440
N19	滝	taki	waterfall	water, dragon	3a10.8, 661, 2655
N19	電	DEN	electricity	rain, lightning	8d5.2, 2790, 5050
N19	縄	nawa, JŌ	rope	thread, sun, (lightning)	6a9.1, 1388, 3617
N20	九	kokono(tsu), KU, KYŪ	nine	grapheme	0a2.15, 3369, 146

N20	究	kiwa(meru), KYŪ	investigate, exhaustible	airhole, nine	3m4.5, 2203, 3314
N20	軌	KI	track	vehicle, nine	7c2.1, 1445, 4610
N20	染	so(maru/meru), shi(miru), SEN	dye	water, nine, tree	4a5.35, 2572, 2240
N20	雜	ZATSU, ZŌ	miscellaneous, mix	nine, tree, chicken	8c6.2, 1385, 5032
N21	枠	waku	frame	wood, 90° angle	4a4.19, 866, 2205
N21	砕	kuda(ku/keru), SAI	break, smash	stone, 90° angle	5a4.6, 1134, 3179
N21	酔	yo(u), SUI	be drunk	wine, 90° angle	7e4.3, 1483, 4781
N21	粋	SUI	essence, purity	rice, 90° angle	6b4.5, 1293, 3467
N22	丸	maru(meru), maru, maru(i), GAN	make round	grapheme	0a3.28, 3417, 155
N22	執	to(ru), SHITSU, SHŪ	take, seize	happiness, round	3b8.15, 1680, 1097
N22	勢	ikio(i), SEI	power	earth, legs, earth, round, power	2g11.6, 2857, 735

N22	熱	atsu(i), NETSU	hot, fever	earth, legs, earth, round, cooking fire	4d11.4, 2866, 2797
N22	熟	u(reru), JUKU	mature	enjoy, round, cooking fire	4d10.5, 2868, 2795
N22	塾	JUKU	private school	enjoy, round, earth	3b10.7, 2860, 1133
N23	犯	oka(su), HAN	commit a crime	watchdog, characteristic	3g2.1, 196, 2869
N23	範	HAN	model, limit	bamboo, vehicle, characteristic	6f9.3, 2709, 3424
N23	厄	YAKU	misfortune	cliff, characteristic	2p2.3, 2947, 816
N23	危	abu(nai), aya(ui), KI	dangerous	tied up, cliff, characteristic	2n4.3, 3199, 187
N24	把	HA	grip	hand, snake	3c4.5, 249, 1846
N24	肥	ko(eru/yasu), HI	fatten, fertilizer	part of the body, snake	4b4.5, 879, 3740
N24	色	iro, SHOKU, HIKI	color, *lust*	tied up, snake	2n4.1, 2029, 3889
N24	絶	ta(tsu/yasu), ZETSU	die out (vi), eradicate (vt)	thread, lust	6a6.11, 1353, 3539

N25	池	ike, CHI	pond	water, wriggle	3a3.4, 218, 2489
N25	地	JI, CHI	ground, place	earth, wriggle	3b3.1, 204, 1056
N25	他	TA	other	human being, wriggle	2a3.4, 35, 361
N25	施	hodoko(su), SHI, SE	give alms, conduct	direction, human, wriggle	4h5.1, 891, 2085
O1	止	to(maru/meru), SHI	stop	grapheme	2m2.2, 2941, 2429
O1	祉	SHI	blessedness	altar, stop	4e4.1, 876, 3232
O1	歯	ha, SHI	*tooth*	stop, rice, container	6b6.11, 2476, 5428
O1	雌	mesu, SHI	female	stop, crouch, chicken	3c6.1, 1055, 2435
O1	歴	REKI	passing of time	cliff, forest, stop	2p12.4, 3019, 835
O1	肯	KŌ	assent	stop, part of the body	4b4.11, 2417, 2432
O1	渋	shibu(ru), shibu(i), JŪ	hesitate, astringent	water, stop, very much	3a8.19, 513, 2600

O2	歩	aru(ku), ayu(mu), HO, BU	walk	grapheme	3n5.3, 2416, 2433
O2	渉	SHŌ	cross over	water, walk	3a8.20, 526, 2591
O2	頻	HIN	frequently	walk, head	9a8.2, 1758, 5128
O3	延	no(biru/basu), EN	extend, postpone	grapheme	2q5.4, 3073, 1547
O3	誕	TAN	birth	words, extend	7a7.15, 1579, 4386
O4	卸	oro(su)	wholesale	grapheme	2e7.1, 1447, 812
O4	御	on, GO, GYO	honorific prefix	step, wholesale	3i9.1, 577, 1628
O5	正	tada(su), masa, SEI, SHŌ	correct, right, regular	grapheme	2m3.3, 3484, 27
O5	政	matsurigoto, SEI, SHŌ	political administration	correct, teacher	4i5.1, 1142, 2045
O5	征	SEI	conquer	step, correct	3i5.3, 293, 1603
O5	証	SHŌ	prove, certificate	words, correct	7a5.5, 1506, 4341

O5	症	SHŌ	illness	sickness, correct	5i5.4, 3280, 3039
O5	整	totono(u/eru), SEI	put in order	bundle, teacher, correct	4i12.3, 2871, 2436
O6	定	sada(maru/meru), TEI, JŌ	*determine*, regular	house, constant	3m5.8, 2229, 1296
O6	錠	JŌ	lock, pill	metal, determine	8a8.12, 1737, 4874
O6	従	shitaga(u/eru), JŪ	*follow*, be attended by	step, (horns), constant	3i7.3, 415, 1613
O6	縦	tate, JŪ	vertical	thread, follow	6a10.2, 1408, 3597
O7	旋	SEN	rotate	direction, human, dance	4h7.2, 957, 2091
O7	婿	muko, SEI	son-in-law	woman, dance, part of the body	3e9.3, 566, 1239
O7	礎	ishizue, SO	foundation stone	stone, forest, dance	5a13.2, 1248, 3222
O7	疑	utaga(u), GI	*doubt*	crouch, arrow, typical, dance	2m12.1, 1565, 755
O7	擬	GI	imitate	hand, doubt	3c14.2, 788, 2026

O7	凝	ko(ru/rasu), GYŌ	congeal, concentrate	ice, doubt	2b14.1, 175, 652
O7	疎	uto(mu), uto(i), SO	shun, estranged	(dance), bundle	0a11.4, 1178, 3021
O8	足	ta(riru/su), ashi, SOKU	suffice, foot	grapheme	7d0.1, 2188, 4546
O8	促	unaga(su)	hasten, urge	human being, suffice	2a7.3, 103, 444
O9	走	hashi(ru), SŌ	run	grapheme	3b4.9, 2194, 4539
O9	徒	TO	follower	step, run	3i7.1, 416, 1514
O9	赴	omomu(ku), FU	proceed to	run, divining rod	3b6.14, 3303, 4540
O9	超	ko(su), ko(eru), CHŌ	surpass	run, summon	3b9.18, 3313, 4543
O10	是	ZE	fair, just	grapheme	4c5.9, 2436, 2120
O10	堤	tsutsumi, TEI	dike, bank	earth, fair	3b9.7, 560, 1108
O10	提	TEI	present, submit	hand, fair	3c9.4, 591, 1967

O10	題	DAI	topic, title	fair, head	9a9.7, 3337, 2164
P1	水	mizu, SUI	water	grapheme	3a0.1, 10, 2482
P1	氷	kō(ru), hi, HYŌ	freeze, ice	drop, (water)	3a1.2, 39, 131
P1	泉	izumi, SEN	*spring*, well	white, water	3a5.33, 2567, 3099
P1	線	SEN	line	thread, spring	6a9.7, 1392, 3580
P1	踏	fu(mu), fu(maeru), TŌ	step on, trample on	foot, water, sun	7d8.3, 1587, 4571
P1	蒸	mu(su), JŌ	evaporate, steam	flower, finish, (water), one, cooking fire	3k9.19, 2334, 4002
P1	承	uketamawa(ru), SHŌ	(humble) hear, agree	finish, three, (water)	0a7.7, 16, 197
P2	永	naga(i), EI	eternal	grapheme	3a1.1, 1937, 130
P2	泳	oyo(gu), EI	swim	water, eternal	3a5.14, 327, 2520
P2	詠	yo(mu), EI	compose poetry	words, eternal	7a5.14, 1500, 4336

P3	求	moto(meru), KYŪ	seek	grapheme	2b5.5, 3550, 137
P3	球	tama, KYŪ	ball	king, seek	4f7.2, 969, 2941
P3	救	suku(u), KYŪ	save	seek, teacher	4i7.1, 1497, 2051
P3	暴	aba(reru), aba(ku), BŌ	*act violently*, disclose a secret	sun, joint, (water)	4c11.2, 2515, 2157
P3	爆	BAKU	explosion	fire, act violently	4d15.2, 1101, 2818
P3	様	sama, YŌ	formal title, mode	tree, lamb's wool, (water)	4a10.25, 1052, 2341
P4	還	KAN	return	net, one, mouth, far, traveler	2q13.4, 3180, 4750
P4	環	KAN	ring, surrounding	king, net, one, mouth, far	4f13.1, 1090, 2970
P4	旅	tabi, RYO	travel	direction, human, (far)	4h6.4, 922, 2088
P4	衆	SHŪ	multitude	blood, drop, drop, (far)	5h7.1, 2683, 4210
P4	園	sono, EN	park	enclosed, earth, mouth, far	3s10.1, 3156, 1047

P4	遠	tō(i), EN	distant	earth, mouth, far, traveler	2q10.4, 3150, 4733
P4	猿	saru, EN	monkey	watchdog, earth, mouth, (far)	3g10.3, 669, 2905
P5	哀	awa(remu), AI	*pity*, sorrow	cap, mouth, grief	2j7.4, 2068, 304
P5	衰	otoro(eru), SUI	decline, wane	pity, one	2j8.1, 2100, 312
P5	衷	CHŪ	inner heart	one, mouth, halve, grief	0a9.9, 2575, 110
P5	表	arawa(reru/su), omote, HYŌ	express, *surface*, table	cultivate, grief	0a8.6, 2429, 108
P5	俵	tawara, HYŌ	straw sack	human being, surface	2a8.21, 115, 467
P5	裏	ura, RI	rear	cap, countryside, grief	2j11.2, 2138, 327
P5	褒	ho(meru), HŌ	commend, praise	cap, (preserve), grief	2j13.1, 2144, 331
P6	壌	JŌ	arable soil	earth, complicated	3b13.4, 755, 1143
P6	譲	yuzu(ru), JŌ	transfer, cede	words, complicated	7a13.1, 1649, 4446

P6	嬢	JŌ	daughter	woman, complicated	3e13.1, 758, 1257
P6	醸	JŌ	brew	wine, complicated	7e13.1, 1654, 4804
P7	衣	koromo, I	clothes	grapheme	5e0.1, 2013, 4214
P7	依	I	dependence	human being, clothes	2a6.1, 84, 426
P7	製	SEI	manufacture	system, clothes	5e8.9, 2803, 4249
P7	懐	natsuka(shii), KAI	long for	feeling, ten, net, clothes	4k13.9, 763, 1782
P7	壊	kowa(su/reru), KAI	break down (vi, vt)	earth, ten, net, clothes	3b13.3, 756, 1147
P7	装	yosō(u), SŌ, SHŌ	dress, wear	vigorous, clothes	5e6.8, 2685, 4234
P8	喪	mo, SŌ	mourning	ten, mouth, mouth, grief	3b9.20, 2825, 117
P9	長	naga(i), CHŌ	long, chief	grapheme	0a8.2, 2556, 4938
P9	張	ha(ru), CHŌ	spread, strain	bow, long	3h8.1, 474, 1570

P9	帳	CHŌ	notebook	cloth, long	3f8.2, 473, 1478
P9	脹	CHŌ	swell	part of the body, long	4b8.1, 1003, 3782
P10	唇	kuchibiru, SHIN	lip	tremble, mouth	3d7.12, 2737, 4654
P10	振	fu(ru), SHIN	swing, shake	hand, tremble	3c7.14, 430, 1920
P10	娠	SHIN	become pregnant	woman, tremble	3e7.10, 408, 1220
P10	震	furu(eru), SHIN	tremble, earthquake	rain, tremble	8d7.3, 2806, 5055
P10	農	NŌ	*farming*	bend, tremble	2p11.1, 2698, 4658
P10	濃	ko(i), NŌ	thick, concentrated	water, farming	3a13.7, 777, 2711
P10	辱	hazukashi(meru), JOKU	humiliate, disgrace	tremble, a bit of	2p8.2, 2736, 4655
P11	氏	uji, SHI	family name, courtesy title	grapheme	0a4.25, 2951, 2478
P11	紙	kami, SHI	paper	thread, family	6a4.4, 1302, 3510

P11	婚	KON	marriage	woman, family, sun	3e8.4, 470, 1236
P12	低	hiku(i), TEI	low	human being, low	2a5.15, 73, 406
P12	抵	TEI	resist	hand, low	3c5.18, 319, 1878
P12	邸	TEI	residence	low, city wall	2d5.10, 1131, 4759
P12	底	soko, TEI	bottom	building, low	3q5.3, 3084, 1508
P13	民	tami, MIN	people	grapheme	0a5.23, 3036, 25
P13	眠	nemu(ru), nemu(i), MIN	sleep, sleepy	eye, people	5c5.2, 1147, 3132
P14	以	I	prefix to increase	grapheme	0a5.1, 41, 348
P14	似	ni(ru), JI	resemble	human being, increase	2a5.11, 63, 376
P15	留	to(maru/meru), RYŪ	stay (vi), keep in place (vt)	outside, rice field	5f5.4, 2580, 3003
P15	貿	BŌ	trade	outside, money	7b5.8, 2601, 4499

P16	仰	ao(gu), ō(se), GYŌ	look up	human being, protector	2a4.10, 48, 375
P16	抑	osa(eru), YOKU	suppress	hand, protector	3c4.12, 257, 1851
P16	迎	muka(eru), GEI	welcome	protector, traveler	32q4.4, 3059, 4669
P16	卵	tamago, RAN	egg	(protector), drop, drop	2e5.2, 849, 199
P16	柳	yanagi, RYŪ	willow	tree, protector	4a5.12, 899, 2233
Q1	仏	hotoke, BUTSU, FUTSU	Buddha, France	human being, oneself	2a2.5, 19, 351
Q1	払	hara(u), FUTSU	pay	hand, oneself	3c2.2, 194, 1828
Q1	私	watashi, SHI	I, private	rice seedling, oneself	5d2.2, 1115, 3265
Q1	窓	mado, SŌ	window	airhole, oneself, heart	3m8.7, 2294, 3326
Q1	離	hana(reru/su), RI	separate	cap, evil, cavity, oneself, chicken	8c10.3, 1836, 5040
Q1	強	tsuyo(i), KYŌ, GŌ	strong	bow, oneself, insect	3h8.3, 475, 1571

Q1	弁	BEN	dialect	oneself, flexible	0a5.30, 2004, 844
Q1	参	mai(ru), SAN	*visit a holy place*	oneself, big, style	3j5.1, 2066, 850
Q1	惨	miji(me), SAN, ZAN	miserable, cruel	feeling, visit a holy place	4k8.5, 481, 1713
Q2	台	DAI, TAI	platform, counter for vehicles	grapheme	3d2.11, 2005, 848
Q2	胎	TAI	womb, uterus	part of the body, platform	4b5.10, 918, 3750
Q2	怠	nama(keru), okota(ru), TAI	be lazy, neglect	platform, heart	4k5.21, 2085, 851
Q2	治	osa(maru/meru), nao(ru/su), JI, CHI	govern, cure	water, platform	3a5.28, 335, 2528
Q2	始	haji(maru/meru), SHI	begin	woman, platform	3e5.9, 281, 1208
Q3	能	NŌ	ability	grapheme	4b6.15, 1323, 853
Q3	態	TAI	attitude, state	ability, heart	4k10.14, 2847, 1743
Q3	罷	HI	dismiss	net, ability	5g10.2, 2617, 3649

Q4	広	hiro(garu/geru), hiro(i), KŌ	broaden (vi, vt), wide	grapheme	3q2.1, 3035, 1499
Q4	鉱	KŌ	ore, mine	metal, wide	8a5.15, 1709, 4843
Q4	拡	KAKU	expansion	hand, wide	3c5.25, 309, 1876
Q5	伝	tsuta(waru/eru), DEN	be transmitted (vi), transmit (vt)	human being, cloud	2a4.14, 44, 379
Q5	転	koro(garu/gasu), koro(bu), TEN	roll over (vi), roll (vt), tumble over	vehicle, cloud	7c4.3, 1480, 4615
Q5	芸	GEI	art	flower, cloud	3k4.12, 2209, 3908
Q5	雲	kumo, UN	cloud	rain, cloud	8d4.1, 2773, 5046
Q5	曇	kumo(ru), DON	become cloudy	sun, rain, cloud	4c12.1, 2521, 2160
Q6	至	ita(ru), SHI	arrive, lead to	grapheme	3b3.6, 2182, 3845
Q6	室	SHITSU	room	house, arrive	3m6.4, 2254, 1300
Q6	窒	CHITSU	plug up, obstruct	airhole, arrive	3m8.9, 2288, 3325

Q6	致	ita(su), CHI	do humbly	arrive, teacher	4i6.2, 1316, 3847
Q6	到	TŌ	*arrival*	arrive, sword	2f6.4, 1264, 3846
Q6	倒	tao(reru/su), TŌ	topple (vi), bring down (vt)	human being, arrival	2a8.5, 124, 487
Q7	去	sa(ru), KYO, KO	go away	grapheme	3b2.2, 2156, 1051
Q7	法	HŌ, HA	law, method	water, go away	3a5.20, 333, 2535
Q7	却	KYAKU	*withdraw*	go away, seal	2e5.3, 1118, 808
Q7	脚	ashi, KYAKU	leg	part of the body, withdraw	4b7.3, 974, 3773
Q8	棄	KI	abandon	development, one, mountain, tree	2j11.5, 2137, 326
Q8	流	naga(reru/su), RYŪ	flow (vi), pour (vt), current	water, development, river	3a7.10, 441, 2576
Q8	硫	RYŪ	sulfur	stone, development, river	5a7.3, 1184, 3191
Q9	育	soda(tsu/teru), IKU	grow up (vi), raise (vt)	grapheme	2j6.4, 2050, 296

Q9	徹	TETSU	go through	step, raise, teacher	3i12.2, 726, 1637
Q9	撤	TETSU	withdraw	hand, raise, teacher	3c12.3, 734, 1999
Q10	充	a(teru), JŪ	allot, fill	grapheme	2j4.5, 2014, 289
Q10	銃	JŪ	gun	metal, fill	8a6.9, 1723, 4854
Q10	統	TŌ	control, comprehensive	thread, fill	6a6.10, 1352, 3536
Q11	鬼	oni, KI	devil	grapheme	5f5.6, 2657, 5276
Q11	塊	katamari, KAI	lump	earth, devil	3b10.2, 632, 1122
Q11	魂	tamashii, KON	soul	cloud, devil	5f9.2, 1063, 5278
Q11	醜	miniku(i), SHŪ	ugly	wine, devil	7e10.1, 1629, 4798
Q11	魔	MA	demon	hemp, devil	3q18.2, 3187, 5398
Q11	魅	MI	charm	devil, not yet	5f10.1, 3329, 5280

Q12	核	KAKU	nucleus	tree, kernel	4a6.22, 927, 2254
Q12	刻	kiza(mu), KOKU	engrave, point of time	kernel, sword	2f6.7, 1267, 681
Q12	劾	GAI	expose a crime	kernel, power	2g6.1, 1266, 721
Q12	該	GAI	correspond to	words, kernel	7a6.10, 1519, 4349
Q13	幼	osana(i), YŌ	very young	fiber, power	2g3.3, 191, 1495
Q13	擁	YŌ	support	hand, cap, (fiber), chicken	3c13.5, 770, 2013
Q13	郷	KYŌ, GŌ	*hometown*	(fiber), (solid), city wall	2d8.14, 549, 4766
Q13	響	hibi(ku), KYŌ	reverberate	hometown, sound	4c15.3, 2878, 5114
Q14	滋	JI	nourish	water, horns, strengthen	3a9.27, 602, 2626
Q14	磁	JI	magnet	stone, horns, strengthen	5a9.6, 1214, 3209
Q14	慈	itsuku(shimu), JI	love, be affectionate to	horns, strengthen, heart	2o11.1, 2339, 612

Q14	幽	YŪ	faint, dim	(strengthen), halve, container	3o6.6, 3008, 112
Q15	玄	GEN	profound	grapheme	2j3.2, 1991, 2918
Q15	弦	tsuru, GEN	string	bow, profound	3h5.1, 287, 1568
Q15	畜	CHIKU	*livestock*	profound, rice field	2j8.7, 2096, 2920
Q15	蓄	takuwa(eru), CHIKU	store up	flower, livestock	3k10.16, 2333, 4024
Q15	率	hiki(iru), SOTSU, RITSU	lead, rate	profound, very much, ten	2j9.1, 2118, 319
Q16	糸	ito, SHI	thread	grapheme	6a0.1, 2179, 3492
Q16	累	RUI	cumulative	rice field, thread	5f6.5, 2585, 3006
Q16	索	SAKU	search for	ten, cover, thread	2k8.2, 2455, 782
Q16	素	SO, SU	element, plain	cultivate, thread	6a4.12, 2458, 3511
Q16	紫	murasaki, SHI	purple	stop, crouch, thread	6a6.15, 2688, 3534

Q16	潔	isagiyo(i), KETSU	brave, immaculate	water, cultivate, sword, thread	3a12.10, 744, 2698
Q16	繁	HAN	luxury, thrive	every, teacher, thread	6a10.13, 2853, 3596
Q16	維	I	*maintenance*, fiber	thread, chicken	6a8.1, 1370, 3552
Q16	羅	RA	thin silk	net, maintenance	5g14.1, 2622, 3654
Q17	系	KEI	lineage, system	grapheme	6a1.1, 1944, 195
Q17	係	kaka(ru), kakari, KEI	connect, person in charge	human being, lineage	2a7.8, 97, 449
Q17	孫	mago, SON	grandchild	child, lineage	2c7.1, 410, 1273
R1	又	mata	moreover	grapheme	2h0.1, 3351, 855
R1	双	futa, SŌ	set of two	moreover, moreover	2h2.1, 25, 857
R1	桑	kuwa, SŌ	mulberry	moreover, moreover, moreover, tree	2h8.1, 2112, 864
R1	収	osa(maru/meru), SHŪ	take in	(bucket), moreover	2h2.2, 198, 860

R1	捜	saga(su), SŌ	search, look for	hand, report, moreover	3c7.5, 432, 1917
R1	受	u(keru), u(karu), JU	*receive*, pass an examination	caress, cover, moreover	2h6.2, 2421, 2826
R1	授	sazu(karu/keru), JU	be granted (vi), confer (vt)	hand, receive	3c8.15, 492, 1946
R1	度	tabi, DO	*degree*, time	building, leather, moreover	3q6.1, 3100, 1511
R1	渡	wata(ru/su), TO	cross (vi), hand over (vt)	water, degree	3a9.35, 611, 2635
R1	服	FUKU	clothes	part of the body, seal, moreover	4b4.6, 878, 3741
R1	報	muku(iru), HŌ	reward, news	happiness, seal, moreover	3c9.16, 1698, 1114
R1	騒	sawa(gu), SŌ	clamor	horse, moreover, insect	10a8.5, 1835, 5221
R1	漫	MAN	aimless, comic	water, sun, net, moreover	3a11.11, 700, 2683
R1	慢	MAN	arrogant, sluggish	feeling, sun, net, moreover	4k11.8, 686, 1755
R2	取	to(ru), SHU	take	grapheme	6e2.2, 1262, 3699

R2	趣	omomuki, SHU	flavor, purpose	run, take	6e9.1, 3317, 4544
R2	最	motto(mo), SAI	*most*	sun, take	4c8.10, 2472, 2146
R2	撮	to(ru), SATSU	photograph	hand, most	3c12.13, 737, 2001
R3	叔	SHUKU	uncle	grapheme	2h6.1, 1272, 861
R3	淑	SHUKU	graceful	water, uncle	3a8.5, 527, 2592
R3	寂	sabi(shii), sabi, JAKU	lonesome	house, uncle	3m8.2, 2290, 1315
R3	督	TOKU	command, lead	uncle, eye	5c8.9, 2796, 3147
R4	隻	SEKI	one of a pair, counter for ships	grapheme	8c2.1, 2755, 5028
R4	獲	e(ru), KAKU	get, acquire	watchdog, flower, one of a pair	3g13.1, 779, 2912
R4	穫	KAKU	harvest	rice seedling, flower, one of a pair	5d13.4, 1251, 3309
R4	護	GO	protect	words, flower, one of a pair	7a13.3, 1648, 4447

R5	祭	matsu(ru), matsu(ri), SAI	worship, *festival*	grapheme	4e6.3, 2672, 3247
R5	際	kiwa, SAI	verge, occasion	fortress, festival	2d11.1, 714, 5018
R5	察	SATSU	*inspect*, guess	house, festival	3m11.6, 2347, 1334
R5	擦	su(ru/reru), SATSU	rub, chafe	hand, inspect	3c14.5, 790, 2025
R6	没	BOTSU	sink	water, strike	3a4.15, 260, 2506
R6	役	YAKU, EKI	service, office, role	step, strike	3i4.2, 244, 1598
R6	疫	EKI	epidemic	sickness, strike	5i4.2, 3276, 3028
R6	投	na(geru), TŌ	throw	hand, strike	3c4.18, 256, 1856
R6	設	mō(keru), SETSU	set up	words, strike	7a4.7, 1471, 4325
R6	殺	koro(su), SATSU	kill	scissors, tree, strike	4a6.35, 1324, 2454
R6	穀	KOKU	cereal	scholar, cover, rice seedling, strike	5d9.4, 1824, 2461

R6	殻	kara, KAKU	shell	scholar, cover, table, strike	3p8.1, 1490, 2456
R6	撃	u(tsu), GEKI	attack	vehicle, strike, hand	3c11.7, 2863, 1986
R6	般	HAN	*in general*, all	ship, strike	6c4.3, 1317, 3865
R6	搬	HAN	carry	hand, in general	3c10.2, 647, 1973
R6	盤	BAN	disk, board	in general, plate	5h10.2, 2851, 3122
R7	怪	aya(shimu), aya(shii), KAI	doubt	feeling, vertical	4k5.11, 297, 1665
R7	径	KEI	path, diameter	step, vertical	3i5.5, 291, 1602
R7	経	he(ru), KEI, KYŌ	pass through, manage	thread, vertical	6a5.11, 1331, 3523
R7	軽	karu(i), KEI	light, easy	vehicle, vertical	7c5.3, 1515, 4620
R7	茎	kuki, KEI	stem	flower, vertical	3k5.23, 2242, 3912
R8	奴	DO	slave, guy	grapheme	3e2.2, 187, 1186

R8	怒	oko(ru), ika(ru), DŌ	get angry	slave, heart	4k5.19, 2571, 1664
R8	努	tsuto(meru), DO	endeavor	slave, power	2g5.6, 2547, 717
R9	反	so(ru/rasu), HAN	bend (vi, vt), against	grapheme	2p2.2, 2945, 817
R9	坂	saka, HAN	slope	earth, against	3b4.7, 234, 1061
R9	板	ita, HAN, BAN	board, plate	wood, against	4a4.21, 858, 2213
R9	販	HAN	sale	money, against	7b4.2, 1477, 4491
R9	飯	meshi, HAN	meal, cooked rice	eat, against	8b4.5, 1691, 5158
R9	仮	kari, KA	temporary	human being, against	2a4.15, 50, 382
R9	返	kae(ru/su), HEN	be restored to (vi), return (vt)	against, traveler	2q4.5, 3060, 4670
R10	支	sasa(eru), SHI	support, branch	grapheme	2k2.1, 1979, 2039
R10	枝	eda, SHI	branch	wood, branch	4a4.18, 863, 2211

R10	肢	SHI	limb	part of the body, branch	4b4.7, 882, 3736
R10	技	waza, GI	skill	hand, branch	3c4.16, 248, 1853
R10	岐	KI	forking road	mountain, branch	3o4.1, 241, 1410
R10	鼓	tsuzumi, KO	drum	good luck, horns, branch	3p10.2, 1786, 5415
R11	皮	kawa, HI	skin	grapheme	2h3.1, 3037, 3109
R11	彼	kare, HI	third person pronoun	step, skin	3i5.2, 290, 1604
R11	披	HI	open	hand, skin	3c5.13, 305, 1874
R11	被	kōmu(ru), HI	get, receive	robe, skin	5e5.3, 1163, 4225
R11	疲	tsuka(reru), HI	tired	sickness, skin	5i5.2, 3278, 3040
R11	破	yabu(reru/ru), HA	tear, rip	stone, skin	5a5.1, 1150, 3186
R11	波	nami, HA	*wave*	water, skin	3a5.9, 330, 2529

R11	婆	BA	old woman	wave, woman	3e8.9, 2762, 1234
S1	喚	KAN	outcry	mouth, trade	3d9.19, 550, 958
S1	換	ka(waru/eru), KAN	be exchanged (vi), exchange (vt)	hand, trade	3c9.15, 587, 1964
S2	免	manuka(reru), MEN	escape from	grapheme	2n6.1, 2067, 573
S2	晩	BAN	evening	sun, escape from	4c8.3, 979, 2145
S2	勉	BEN	endeavor	escape from, power	2n8.1, 3318, 228
S2	逸	ITSU	let slip	escape from, traveler	2q8.6, 3120, 4708
S3	陶	TŌ	pottery	fortress, envelope, can	2d8.11, 546, 5003
S3	胸	mune, KYŌ	chest	part of the body, envelope, evil	4b6.9, 951, 3768
S3	濁	nigo(ru/su), DAKU	become turbid (vi), make turbid (vt)	water, net, envelope, insect	3a13.8, 774, 2710
S3	菊	KIKU	chrysanthemum	flower, envelope, rice	3k8.30, 2303, 3981

S3	匁	monme	unit of weight (3.75 g)	envelope, (scissors)	0a4.38, 3465, 159
S4	勺	SHAKU	unit of capacity (18 ml) (grapheme:scoop)	grapheme	0a3.5, 2933, 740
S4	酌	SHAKU	pour wine	wine, scoop	7e3.3, 1461, 4778
S4	約	YAKU	approximately, promise	thread, scoop	6a3.7, 1280, 3499
S4	的	mato, TEKI	target, adjectival suffix	white, scoop	4c4.12, 1125, 3097
S4	釣	tsu(ru)	angle	metal, scoop	8a3.5, 1674, 4820
S4	均	KIN	even	earth, envelope, ice	3b4.8, 235, 1065
S5	句	KU	phrase, haiku	grapheme	3d2.13, 2967, 745
S5	拘	KŌ	arrest	hand, phrase	3c5.28, 310, 1881
S5	敬	uyama(u), KEI	*respect*	flower, phrase, teacher	4i8.4, 1701, 2055
S5	警	KEI	warn	respect, words	7a12.7, 2893, 4439

S6	旬	JUN	ten-day period	grapheme	4c2.5, 2978, 747
S7	喝	KATSU	hoarse	mouth, dry up	3d8.8, 461, 953
S7	渇	kawa(ku), KATSU	be thirsty	water, dry up	3a8.13, 515, 2596
S7	褐	KATSU	brown	robe, dry up	5e8.7, 1210, 4254
S7	謁	ETSU	audience	words, dry up	7a8.6, 1570, 4382
S7	掲	kaka(geru)	put up a sign	hand, dry up	3c8.13, 494, 1934
S8	物	mono, BUTSU, MOTSU	thing	cattle, never	4g4.2, 874, 2857
S8	易	yasa(shii), EKI, I	*easy*, trade	sun, never	4c4.9, 2411, 2107
S8	賜	tamawa(ru), SHI	award, bestow	money, easy	7b8.2, 1585, 4514
S9	万	MAN, BAN	ten thousand	grapheme	0a3.8, 2936, 7
S9	励	hage(mu/masu)	strive for (vi), encourage (vt)	cliff, ten thousand, power	2g5.4, 1119, 193

S9	別	waka(reru), BETSU	separate, another	mouth, ten thousand, sword	2f5.3, 1117, 674
S10	腸	CHŌ	intestines	part of the body, heat	4b9.8, 1033, 3798
S10	揚	a(garu/geru), YŌ	be up (vi), raise high (vt)	hand, heat	3c9.5, 593, 1966
S10	陽	YŌ	sun, positive	fortress, heat	2d9.5, 626, 5012
S10	湯	yu, TŌ	hot water	water, heat	3a9.23, 612, 2633
S10	場	ba, JŌ	place	earth, heat	3b9.6, 558, 1113
S10	傷	ita(mu/meru), kizu, SHŌ	hurt (vi), injure (vt)	human being, human, heat	2a11.10, 158, 535
S11	象	SHŌ, ZŌ	*phenomenon*, elephant	tied up, mouth, halve, (pork belly)	2n10.1, 2134, 4472
S11	像	ZŌ	image, statue	human being, phenomenon	2a12.8, 166, 540
S11	塚	tsuka	mound	earth, cover, pork belly	3b9.10, 556, 1120
S11	豚	buta, TON	pig, pork	part of the body, pork belly	4b7.2, 976, 3772

S11	逐	CHIKU	follow, drive out	pork belly, traveler	2q7.6, 3102, 4696
S11	豪	GŌ	magnificent, powerful	watchtower, cover, pork belly	2j12.3, 2140, 329
S11	劇	GEKI	drama	tiger, pork belly, sword	2f13.2, 1904, 247
S12	家	ie, ya, KA, KE	house, home	grapheme	3m7.1, 2273, 1311
S12	稼	kase(gu), KA	work, earn money	rice seedling, home	5d10.3, 1230, 3301
S12	嫁	totsu(gu), yome, KA	marry, bride	woman, home	3e10.6, 635, 1249
S13	隊	TAI	*squad*, army unit	fortress, boar	2d9.7, 625, 5010
S13	墜	TSUI	fall	squad, earth	3b11.7, 2881, 1132
S13	遂	to(geru), SUI	accomplish	boar, traveler	2q9.13, 3138, 4716
S14	墾	KON	open up farmland	intimate, earth	3b13.6, 2896, 1142
S14	懇	nengo(ro), KON	friendly, familiar	intimate, heart	4k13.12, 2899, 1781

S15	欠	ka(keru/ku), KETSU	lack	grapheme	4j0.1, 1987, 2412
S15	吹	fu(ku), SUI	blow	mouth, lack	3d4.3, 231, 901
S15	炊	ta(ku), SUI	cook	fire, lack	4d4.1, 870, 2752
S15	飲	no(mu), IN	drink	eat, lack	8b4.1, 1692, 5159
S15	軟	yawa(raka), NAN	soft	vehicle, lack	7c4.1, 1479, 4614
S15	款	KAN	article, goodwill	scholar, show, lack	4j8.2, 1700, 2418
S15	欺	azamu(ku), GI	betray	game, lack	4j8.1, 1703, 2419
S15	歌	uta(u), uta, KA	sing, song	possibility, possibility, lack	4j10.2, 1825, 2422
S15	歓	KAN	pleasure	eagle, lack	4j11.1, 1867, 2425
S16	次	tsu(gu), tsugi, JI, SHI	be next, next	grapheme	2b4.1, 54, 638
S16	資	SHI	capital	next, money	7b6.7, 2695, 4510

S16	姿	sugata, SHI	figure	next, woman	3e6.10, 2636, 1215
S16	諮	haka(ru), SHI	consult	words, next, mouth	7a9.4, 1596, 4404
S16	盗	nusu(mu), TŌ	steal	next, plate	5h6.2, 2670, 3115
S17	夕	yū, SEKI	evening	grapheme	0a3.14, 3387, 1167
S17	多	ō(i), TA	*many*	evening, evening	0a6.5, 2170, 1169
S17	移	utsu(ru/su), I	move (vi), shift (vt)	rice seedling, many	5d6.1, 1177, 3282
S17	外	hazu(reru/su), soto, GAI,GE	be separated, outside	evening, divining rod	2m3.1, 186, 2268
S17	夢	yume, MU	dream	flower, net, cover, evening	3k10.14, 2336, 4028
S17	腕	ude, WAN	arm, skill	part of the body, house, evening, characteristic	4b8.6, 1006, 3786
S18	傑	KETSU	outstanding	human being, opposition, tree	2a11.6, 155, 517
S18	隣	tonari, RIN	neighbor	fortress, rice, opposition	2d13.1, 781, 5023

S18	瞬	matata(ku), SHUN	blink, instant	eye, caress, cover, opposition	5c13.1, 1247, 3159
S19	名	na, MEI, MYŌ	name	grapheme	3d3.12, 2169, 1170
S19	銘	MEI	inscription	metal, name	8a6.4, 1724, 4852
S20	殊	koto, SHU	special	death, vermilion	0a10.7, 942, 2443
S20	殉	JUN	martyr	death, ten-day period	4c6.9, 941, 2444
S20	死	shi(nu)	*die*	die, crouch	0a6.6, 3521, 2439
S20	葬	hōmu(ru), SŌ	bury	flower, die, flexible	3k9.15, 2320, 4000
S21	列	RETSU	row	grapheme	2f4.4, 824, 2438
S21	烈	RETSU	vehement	row, cooking fire	4d6.3, 2652, 2761
S21	裂	sa(ku/keru), RETSU	split (vi, vt)	row, clothes	5e6.7, 2687, 4233
S21	例	tato(eru), REI	give an example, example, custom	human being, row	2a6.7, 89, 428

S22	久	hisa(shii), KYŪ	long duration	grapheme	0a3.7, 3384, 153
S22	畝	se, une	ridge	cap, rice field, long duration	5f5.5, 1465, 311
S23	冬	fuyu, TŌ	*winter*	march, ice	4i2.1, 2157, 1161
S23	終	o(waru/eru), SHŪ	end	thread, winter	6a5.9, 1336, 3521
S23	条	JŌ	article	march, tree	4i4.1, 2200, 1164
S23	隆	RYŪ	prosper	fortress, march, life	2d8.6, 545, 4999
S23	降	o(riru/rosu), fu(ru), KŌ	descend, rain	fortress, march, barrier	2d7.7, 458, 4994
S23	峰	mine, HŌ	peak	mountain, march, three, halve	3o7.6, 411, 1423
S23	縫	nu(u), HŌ	sew	thread, march, three, halve, traveler	6a9.15, 1406, 3582
S23	麦	mugi, BAKU	wheat	cultivate, march	4i4.2, 2408, 5385
S23	変	ka(waru/eru), HEN	change	pink, march	2j7.3, 2069, 306

S23	夏	natsu, KA	summer	one, nose, march	4i7.5, 2113, 58
S23	後	ato, ushi(ro), GO, KŌ	after, later, behind	step, fiber, march	3i6.5, 361, 1610
S23	愛	AI	love	caress, cover, heart, march	4i10.1, 2492, 2829
S23	処	SHO	*treat*, dispose	march, table	4i2.2, 3031, 1162
S23	拠	KYO, KO	based on	hand, treat	3c5.26, 321, 1871
S23	夜	yoru, yo, YA	*night*	cap, human being, (march), drop	2j6.1, 2056, 298
S23	液	EKI	liquid	water, night	3a8.29, 511, 2599
S24	複	FUKU	double, compound	robe, fold	5e9.3, 1222, 4255
S24	腹	hara, FUKU	belly	part of the body, fold	4b9.4, 1034, 3800
S24	復	FUKU	*repeat*	step, fold	3i9.4, 575, 1627
S24	覆	kutsugae(ru/su), ō(u), FUKU	overturn (vi, vt), cover	west, repeat	4c14.6, 2726, 4279

S25	唆	sosonoka(su), SA	instigate, incite	mouth, stimulate	3d7.8, 402, 925
S25	俊	SHUN	brilliant	human being, stimulate	2a7.10, 102, 448
S25	酸	SAN	acid, oxygen	wine, stimulate	7e7.2, 1563, 4789
S25	陵	misasagi, RYŌ	imperial tomb	fortress, earth, legs, march	2d8.5, 544, 4998
S26	各	onoono, KAKU	each	grapheme	4i3.3, 2168, 1163
S26	格	KAKU	status, norm	tree, each	4a6.17, 926, 2259
S26	閣	KAKU	cabinet	gate, each	8e6.3, 3327, 4957
S26	客	KYAKU, KAKU	*guest*, visitor	house, each	3m6.3, 2250, 1302
S26	額	hitai, GAKU	forehead, amount	guest, head	9a9.6, 1805, 5136
S26	略	RYAKU	abridged, strategy	rice field, each	5f6.4, 1169, 3007
S26	酪	RAKU	dairy product	wine, each	7e6.4, 1538, 4786

S26	絡	kara(maru/mu), RAKU	entwine, get entangled	thread, each	6a6.6, 1351, 3533
S26	落	o(chiru/tosu), RAKU	fall (vi), drop (vt)	flower, water, each	3k9.13, 2318, 4003
S26	路	ji, RO	*road*	foot, each	7d6.5, 1533, 4561
S26	露	tsuyu, RO	dew, expose, Russia	rain, road	8d13.1, 2818, 5069
T1	登	nobo(ru), TŌ, TO	*climb*	volcano, bean	8d9.26, 2595, 3094
T1	澄	su(mu/masu), CHŌ	become clear (vi), make clear (vt)	water, climb	3a12.11, 740, 2699
T1	発	HATSU, HOTSU	*start*, emit	volcano, two, legs	0a9.5, 2565, 3092
T1	廃	suta(reru), HAI	get out of use, abolish, waste	building, start	3q9.3, 3146, 1526
T2	会	a(u), KAI, E	*meet*, society	roof, cloud	2a4.19, 2020, 381
T2	絵	KAI, E	picture	thread, meet	6a6.8, 1346, 3537
T2	診	mi(ru), SHIN	examine a patient	words, roof, style	7a5.9, 1504, 4338

T2	珍	mezura(shii), CHIN	rare	king, roof, style	4f5.6, 909, 2933
T2	全	matta(ku), ZEN	*whole*	roof, king	2a4.16, 2022, 384
T2	栓	SEN	stopper, plug	wood, whole	4a6.26, 934, 2247
T2	茶	CHA, SA	tea	flower, roof, (wood)	3k6.19, 2259, 3940
T2	漆	urushi, SHITSU	lacquer	water, wood, roof, (water)	3a11.10, 704, 2679
T2	企	kuwada(teru), KI	plan, project	roof, stop	2a4.17, 2021, 373
T2	傘	kasa, SAN	umbrella	roof, (4x) human being, ten	2a10.7, 2131, 518
T2	幹	miki, KAN	trunk	fog, roof, dry	4c9.8, 1718, 790
T3	介	KAI	be in between, mediate	grapheme	2a2.9, 1967, 347
T3	界	KAI	world, bounds	rice field, be in between	5f4.7, 2563, 2998
T4	余	ama(ru/su), YO	remain over (vi), leave over (vt),excess	grapheme	2a5.24, 2042, 408

T4	徐	JO	slowly	step, leave over	3i7.2, 414, 1612
T4	除	nozo(ku), JO	get rid of, exclude	fortress, leave over	2d7.10, 456, 4993
T4	叙	JO	description	leave over, moreover	2h7.1, 1446, 862
T4	途	TO	on the way	leave over, traveler	2q7.16, 3107, 4697
T4	塗	nu(ru), TO	paint	water, leave over, earth	3b10.10, 2841, 1124
T4	斜	nana(me), SHA	slanting, oblique	leave over, bucket	2a9.21, 1486, 2074
T5	金	kane, KIN, KON	metal, money, gold	grapheme	8a0.1, 2057, 4815
T6	舎	SHA	building	grapheme	2a6.23, 2060, 423
T6	捨	su(teru), SHA	discard	hand, barn	3c8.26, 501, 1944
T6	舗	HO	pave, shop	barn, fishing rod	3b12.4, 1735, 552
T7	食	ta(beru), ku(u), SHOKU	eat	grapheme	8b0.1, 2075, 5154

T7	飾	kaza(ru), SHOKU	decorate	eat, human, cloth	8b5.3, 1717, 5161
T8	令	REI	command	grapheme	2a3.9, 1995, 360
T8	命	inochi, MEI, MYŌ	life, fate	(command), mouth	2a6.26, 2058, 430
T8	冷	hi(eru/yasu), tsume(tai), REI	cool down (vi), chill (vt), cold	ice, command	2b5.3, 80, 642
T8	鈴	suzu, REI, RIN	bell	metal, command	8a5.11, 1710, 4837
T8	零	REI	zero	rain, command	8d5.4, 2792, 5048
T8	齢	REI	age	tooth, command	6b11.5, 1895, 5431
T8	領	RYŌ	govern, rule	command, head	9a5.2, 1224, 5124
T9	今	ima, KON, KIN	now, present	grapheme	2a2.10, 1968, 352
T9	琴	koto, KIN	Japanese harp	king, king, now	4f8.11, 2781, 2949
T9	吟	GIN	recite, sing	mouth, now	3d4.8, 230, 898

T9	念	NEN	special attention	now, heart	2a6.24, 2059, 424
T9	含	fuku(mu/meru), GAN	contain, include	now, mouth	2a5.25, 2041, 402
T9	陰	kage(ru), IN	shade	fortress, now, cloud	2d8.7, 541, 5006
T10	合	a(u/wasu), GŌ, GA	fit (vi), put together (vt)	grapheme	2a4.18, 2019, 383
T10	拾	hiro(u), SHŪ, JŪ	pick up	hand, fit	3c6.14, 379, 1901
T10	給	KYŪ	supply, wage	thread, fit	6a6.7, 1350, 3538
T10	搭	TŌ	load (a vehicle), ride	hand, flower, fit	3c9.10, 592, 1959
T10	塔	TŌ	tower	earth, flower, fit	3b9.9, 561, 1109
T10	答	kota(eru), kota(e), TŌ	answer	bamboo, fit	6f6.12, 2681, 3394
T11	倹	KEN	frugal	human being, check	2a8.27, 116, 479
T11	検	KEN	examination	wood, check	4a8.28, 986, 2304

T11	険	kewa(shii), KEN	steep	fortress, check	2d8.8, 542, 5000
T11	験	KEN	test	horse, check	10a8.4, 1833, 5220
T11	剣	tsurugi, KEN	sword	check, sword	2f8.5, 1672, 696
T12	愉	YU	pleasure	feeling, conversion	4k9.13, 582, 1726
T12	諭	sato(su), YU	admonish	words, conversion	7a9.13, 1598, 4411
T12	輸	YU	transport	vehicle, conversion	7c9.5, 1607, 4634
T12	癒	YU	heal	sickness, conversion, heart	5i13.3, 3291, 3081
T13	倫	RIN	moral	human being, logic	2a8.28, 120, 474
T13	輪	wa, RIN	wheel, ring	vehicle, logic	7c8.4, 1589, 4630
T13	論	RON	thesis, theory	words, logic	7a8.13, 1574, 4391
T14	八	ya(tsu), yat(tsu), HACHI	eight	grapheme	2o0.1, 3, 577

T14	穴	ana, KETSU	hole	house, eight	3m2.2, 2159, 3313
T14	分	wa(keru), wa(karu), BU, BUN, FUN	divide, understand, *part*, minute	eight, sword	2o2.1, 1972, 578
T14	粉	kona, ko, FUN	powder, flour	rice, part	6b4.6, 1291, 3469
T14	紛	magi(reru/rawasu), magi(rawashii), FUN	divert, distract, ambiguous	thread, part	6a4.8, 1296, 3506
T14	雰	FUN	fog	rain, part	8d4.2, 2772, 5045
T14	盆	BON	tray, bon festival	part, plate	2o7.6, 2079, 594
T14	貧	mazu(shii), HIN, BIN	poor	part, money	2o9.5, 2143, 600
T14	頒	HAN	distribution	part, head	9a4.3, 1043, 5119
T15	公	ōyake, KŌ	public	grapheme	2o2.2, 1974, 579
T15	松	matsu, SHŌ	pine	tree, public	4a4.16, 864, 2212
T15	訟	SHŌ	accusation	words, public	7a4.6, 1472, 4320

T15	翁	Ō	old man	public, feather	2o8.6, 2108, 596
T15	総	SŌ	general, total	thread, public, heart	6a8.20, 1379, 3567
T16	沿	so(u), EN	run along, following along	water, run out	3a5.23, 328, 2525
T16	鉛	namari, EN	lead	metal, run out	8a5.14, 1707, 4842
T16	船	fune, SEN	ship	ship, run out	6c5.4, 1341, 3873
T17	谷	tani, KOKU	valley	grapheme	2o5.3, 2043, 4458
T17	浴	a(biru/biseru), YOKU	bathe	water, valley	3a7.18, 445, 2568
T17	欲	hos(suru), YOKU	desire	valley, lack	4j7.1, 1475, 4461
T17	俗	ZOKU	manners, customs	human being, valley	2a7.17, 104, 453
T17	裕	YŪ	abundant	robe, valley	5e7.3, 1195, 4241
T17	容	YŌ	*appearance*	house, valley	3m7.8, 2277, 1309

T17	溶	to(keru/kasu), YŌ	melt (vi), dissolve (vt)	water, appearance	3a10.15, 664, 2659
T18	具	GU	*tool*	eye, stool	5c3.1, 2552, 3128
T18	真	ma, SHIN	*truth*	ten, tool	2k8.1, 2111, 783
T18	慎	tsutsushi(mu), SHIN	be discreet, restrain oneself	feeling, truth	4k10.4, 643, 1742
T18	鎮	shizu(maru/meru), CHIN	get quiet, calm down	metal, truth	8a10.6, 1759, 4903
T18	益	EKI	benefit, profit	horns, (stool), plate	2o8.5, 2285, 597
T18	誉	homa(re), YŌ	honor	gather, stool, words	3n10.1, 2502, 4353
T18	挙	a(garu/geru), KYO	cite, arrest, nominate	gather, stool, hand	3n7.1, 2456, 1902
T18	寒	samu(i), KAN	cold	house, (well), stool, (ice)	3m9.3, 2311, 1322
U1	尿	NYŌ	urine	behind, water	3r4.1, 3064, 1382
U1	尾	o, BI	tail	behind, hair	3r4.2, 3062, 1383

U1	届	todo(ku/keru)	deliver (vt), reach (vi)	behind, reason	3r5.1, 3078, 1385
U1	層	SŌ	layer	behind, augment	3r11.2, 3161, 1402
U1	履	ha(ku), RI	put on shoes	behind, repeat	3r12.1, 3171, 1404
U1	漏	mo(ru/rasu), RŌ	leak, let leak	water, behind, rain	3a11.19, 701, 2682
U1	遅	oku(reru/rasu), CHI	be late, delay	behind, sheep, traveler	2q9.17, 3133, 4722
U1	塀	HEI	fence	earth, behind, (horns), with both hands	3b9.11, 557, 1131
U1	展	TEN	unfold, display	behind, (herbs), mourning	3r7.2, 3111, 1396
U1	殿	tono, dono, DEN, TEN	honorific title, palace	behind, herbs, animal legs, strike	3r10.1, 1792, 242
U1	刷	su(ru), SATSU	print	behind, cloth, sword	2f6.9, 1273, 210
U1	尉	I	*lieutenant*	behind, show, a bit of	4e6.4, 1685, 231
U1	慰	nagusa(mu/meru), I	amuse oneself, comfort	lieutenant, heart	4k11.13, 2867, 1758

U1	居	i(ru), KYO	be present, *reside*	behind, old	3r5.3, 3080, 1387
U1	据	su(eru)	install	hand, reside	3c8.33, 497, 1935
U1	尼	ama, NI	nun	behind, crouch	3r2.2, 3033, 1378
U1	泥	doro, DEI	mud, dirt	water, behind, crouch	3a5.29, 326, 2533
U1	屋	ya, OKU	*small shop*	behind, arrive	3r6.3, 3098, 1392
U1	握	nigi(ru), AKU	grasp	hand, small shop	3c9.17, 585, 1963
U1	属	ZOKU	*belong to*	behind, drop, (insect), cavity	3r9.1, 3145, 1400
U1	嘱	SHOKU	entrust, commission	mouth, belong to	3d12.11, 718, 989
U1	屈	KUTSU	bend, *lean over*	behind, go out	3r5.2, 3079, 1386
U1	掘	ho(ru), KUTSU	dig	hand, lean over	3c8.32, 496, 1943
U1	堀	hori	ditch	earth, lean over	3b8.11, 467, 1095

U2	壁	kabe, HEKI	wall	prison, earth	3b13.7, 2895, 1148
U2	癖	kuse, HEKI	habit	sickness, prison	5i13.2, 3290, 3082
U2	避	sa(keru), HI	avoid	prison, traveler	2q13.3, 3179, 4749
U3	尺	SHAKU	unit of length (30cm) (grapheme: measure)	grapheme	3r1.1, 3440, 1377
U3	釈	SHAKU	explanation	number, measure	6b5.5, 1484, 4809
U3	沢	sawa, TAKU	swamp	water, measure	3a4.18, 267, 2503
U3	択	TAKU	selection	hand, measure	3c4.21, 255, 1845
U3	訳	wake, YAKU	translation	words, measure	7a4.8, 1473, 4327
U3	駅	EKI	station	horse, measure	10a4.4, 1822, 5199
U3	尽	tsu(kiru/kusu), JIN	be exhausted, exhaust	measure, ice	3r3.1, 3050, 1380
U3	昼	hiru, CHŪ	daytime	measure, sunrise	4c5.15, 3097, 53

U3	声	koe, SEI	voice	scholar, (behind), halve	3p4.4, 2198, 1066
U4	戸	to, KO	door	grapheme	4m0.1, 1930, 1817
U4	雇	yato(u), KO	*employ someone*	door, chicken	4m8.1, 1956, 1826
U4	顧	kaeri(miru), KO	look back	employ someone, head	9a12.2, 1900, 5141
U4	所	tokoro, SHO	place, location	door, ax	4m4.3, 851, 1821
U4	炉	RO	furnace	fire, door	4d4.2, 869, 2750
U4	房	fusa, BŌ	tuft room	door, direction	4m4.2, 1946, 1819
U4	啓	KEI	enlightenment	door, teacher, mouth	3d8.17, 2763, 940
U4	肩	kata, KEN	shoulder	door, part of the body	4m4.1, 1947, 1820
U4	扇	ōgi, SEN	fan	door, feather	4m6.1, 1950, 1823
U4	戻	modo(ru/su)	*return* (vi, vt)	door, big	4m3.1, 1942, 1818

U4	涙	namida, RUI	teardrop	water, return	3a7.21, 440, 2569
U5	遍	HEN	all over	enlarge, traveler	2q9.16, 3136, 4718
U5	偏	katayo(ru), HEN	be one-sided	human being, enlarge	2a9.16, 133, 511
U5	編	a(mu), HEN	knit, compile	thread, enlarge	6a9.13, 1387, 3583
U6	倉	kura, SŌ	storehouse	grapheme	2a8.37, 2104, 486
U6	創	SŌ	creation	storehouse, sword	2f10.3, 1815, 702
V1	右	migi, U, YŪ	right	grapheme	3d2.15, 2975, 878
V1	若	waka(i), JAKU	*young*	flower, right	3k5.12, 2241, 3926
V1	諾	DAKU	consent	words, young	7a8.10, 1568, 4383
V2	有	a(ru), YŪ, U	be, have	grapheme	4b2.3, 2983, 3727
V2	賄	makana(u), WAI	bribe	money, have	7b6.1, 1529, 4507

V2	堕	DA	degenerate	fortress, have, earth	3b8.14, 2822, 1092
V2	随	ZUI	follow	fortress, have, traveler	2d8.10, 627, 5004
V2	髄	ZUI	marrow	bone, have, traveler	4b14.3, 1842, 5242
V3	布	nuno, FU	linen, cloth	grapheme	3f2.1, 2973, 1468
V3	怖	kowa(i), FU	scary, frightening	feeling, linen	4k5.6, 296, 1662
V3	希	KI	scarcity	scissors, linen	3f4.1, 2049, 1470
V4	存	SON, ZON	existence	reality, child	2c3.1, 2982, 1267
V4	在	a(ru), ZAI	be in a place, reside in	reality, earth	3b3.8, 2984, 1055
V5	雄	osu, YŪ	male	stable, oneself, chicken	8c4.1, 1008, 5030
V5	丈	take, JŌ	height (3.03 m)	stable, drop	0a3.26, 3419, 151
V5	左	hidari, SA	*left*	stable, handicraft	0a5.20, 2974, 1455

V5	佐	SA	assist	human being, left	2a5.9, 67, 392
V5	惰	DA	laziness	feeling, left, part of the body	4k9.6, 579, 1727
V6	友	tomo, YŪ	friend	grapheme	2h2.3, 2954, 858
V6	抜	nu(keru/ku), BATSU	come out, pull out	hand, friend	3c4.10, 246, 1854
V6	髪	kami, HATSU	hair	(long), style, friend	3j11.3, 2846, 5255
V6	暖	atata(maru/meru), atata(kai), DAN	get warm (vi), warm up (vt)	sun, caress, one, friend	4c9.4, 1011, 2153
V6	援	EN	aid	hand, caress, one, friend	3c9.7, 586, 1961
V6	緩	yuru(mu/meru), yuru(yaka), KAN	slacken (vi), loosen (vt)	thread, caress, one, friend	4a9.8, 1389, 3584
V7	史	SHI	history	grapheme	0a5.38, 3510, 91
V7	吏	RI	*official*, administrator	one, history	0a6.22, 3536, 183
V7	使	tsuka(u), SHI	use, messenger	human being, an official	2a6.2, 90, 432

V8	更	fu(keru/kasu), sara, KŌ	grow late, anew	grapheme	0a7.12, 3541, 42
V8	硬	kata(i), KŌ	hard	stone, grow late	5a7.1, 1183, 3193
V8	便	tayo(ri), BEN, BIN	mail, convenient, post	human being, grow late	2a7.5, 95, 451
V9	大	ō(kii), DAI, TAI	big	grapheme	0a3.18, 3416, 1171
V9	奮	furu(u), FUN	be invigorated	big, chicken, rice field	5f11.2, 2369, 1184
V9	因	yo(ru), IN	be caused by, *cause*	enclosed, big	3s3.2, 3054, 1026
V9	姻	IN	marriage	woman, cause	3e6.8, 353, 1214
V9	恩	ON	grace, gratitude	cause, heart	4k6.23, 2655, 1684
V9	太	futo(ru), futo(i), TAI, TA	fatten, *thick*	big, drop	0a4.18, 2152, 1172
V9	駄	DA	horse load	horse, thick	10a4.1, 1821, 5198
V10	漠	BAKU	desert, obscure	water, concealed	3a10.18, 655, 2649

V10	膜	MAKU	membrane	part of the body, concealed	4b10.6, 1062, 3803
V10	模	MO, BO	pattern, imitate	wood, concealed	4a10.16, 1050, 2345
V10	墓	haka, BO	tomb	concealed, earth	3k10.18, 2332, 4027
V10	暮	ku(reru), ku(rasu), BO	dusk, live	concealed, sun	3k11.14, 2354, 4041
V10	募	tsuno(ru), BO	grow stronger (vi), recruit (vt)	concealed, power	3k9.23, 2316, 3996
V10	幕	MAKU, BAKU	curtain, shogunate	concealed, cloth	3k10.19, 2335, 4026
V10	慕	shita(u), BO	yearn for	concealed, (heart)	3k11.12, 2353, 4040
V11	犬	inu, KEN	dog	grapheme	3g0.1, 3464, 2868
V11	献	KEN	offer, present	south, dog	3g9.6, 1785, 2901
V11	伏	fu(su/seru), FUKU	bend down, lay face down	human being, dog	2a4.1, 45, 377
V11	状	JŌ	condition, letter	bed, dog	2b5.1, 272, 2839

V11	獣	kemono, JŪ	beast	gather, rice field, one, mouth, dog	3g12.3, 1892, 2909
V11	黙	dama(ru), MOKU	become silent	countryside, dog, cooking fire	4d11.5, 2865, 2796
V11	獄	GOKU	prison	watchdog, words, dog	3g11.1, 712, 2906
V11	然	ZEN, NEN	so, *as*, like	part of the body, dog, cooking fire	4d8.10, 2782, 2770
V11	燃	mo(eru/yasu), NEN	burn (vi, vt)	fire, as	4d12.2, 1081, 2808
V12	僚	RYŌ	colleague	human being, recover	2a12.4, 165, 545
V12	療	RYŌ	treatment	sickness, recover	5i12.3, 3288, 3078
V12	寮	RYŌ	dormitory	house, recover	3m12.2, 2359, 1340
V13	天	ame, ama, TEN	heaven, nature	grapheme	0a4.21, 3442, 16
V13	蚕	kaiko, SAN	silkworm	heaven, insect	6d4.8, 2457, 57
V13	添	so(u/eru), TEN	go along with(vi), add to (vt)	water, (heaven), (heart)	3a8.22, 529, 2601

V13	笑	wara(u), e(mu), SHŌ	laugh	bamboo, (heaven)	6f4.1, 2646, 3374
V13	橋	hashi, KYŌ	bridge	wood, (heaven), mouth, cavity, mouth	4a12.8, 1078, 2378
V13	矯	ta(meru), KYŌ	straighten	arrow, (heaven), mouth, cavity, mouth	3d14.5, 1241, 3175
V14	咲	sa(ku)	bloom	mouth, from heaven	3d6.12, 349, 922
V14	朕	CHIN	imperial	part of the body, from heaven	4b6.6, 949, 3757
V14	送	oku(ru), SŌ	send	from heaven, traveler	2q6.9, 3093, 4683
V14	関	seki, KAN	barrier	gate, from heaven	8e6.7, 3328, 4958
V15	夫	otto, FŪ, FU	husband, business man	grapheme	0a4.31, 3460, 164
V15	扶	FU	help	hand, husband	3c4.4, 247, 1850
V15	規	KI	regulation	husband, see	5c6.9, 978, 4285
V15	替	ka(waru/eru), TAI	be replaced (vi), *replace* (vt)	husband, husband, sun	4c8.12, 2783, 2140

V15	潜	mogu(ru), hiso(mu), SEN	dive, lurk	water, replace	3a12.6, 746, 2703
V15	賛	SAN	praise, approve of	husband, husband, money	7b8.6, 2809, 4516
V15	渓	KEI	valley	water, caress, husband	3a8.16, 516, 2581
V15	鶏	niwatori, KEI	chicken	caress, husband, bird, cooking fire	11b8.4, 1768, 5359
V15	僕	BOKU	I (masculine speech), servant	human being, (line up), horns, husband	2a12.1, 164, 544
V15	撲	BOKU	hit	hand, (line up), horns, husband	3c12.1, 733, 1993
V16	漢	KAN	Chinese, fellow	water, difficult	3a10.17, 657, 2662
V16	嘆	nage(ku), TAN	bemoan, lament	mouth, difficult	3d10.8, 630, 974
V16	難	muzuka(shii), kata(i), NAN	difficult	difficult, chicken	8c10.2, 1838, 5038
V17	決	ki(maru/meru), KETSU	be decided (vi), decide (vt)	water, choice	3a4.6, 263, 2509
V17	快	kokoroyo(i), KAI	pleasant	feeling, choice	4k4.2, 245, 1654

V18	央	Ō	center	grapheme	0a5.33, 3509, 86
V18	英	EI	distinguished, England	flower, center	3k5.5, 2238, 3927
V18	映	utsu(ru/su), EI	project, reflect	sun, center	4c5.1, 892, 2118
V19	狭	sema(i), KYŌ	narrow	watchdog, pinch	3g6.2, 396, 2882
V19	峡	KYŌ	gorge	mountain, pinch	3o6.1, 357, 1417
V19	挟	hasa(maru/mu), KYŌ	sandwiched between	hand, pinch	3c6.1, 377, 1915
V20	券	KEN	ticket, certificate	document, sword	2f6.10, 2630, 678
V20	勝	ka(tsu), SHŌ	win, excel	part of the body, document, power	4b8.4, 1005, 3787
V20	謄	TŌ	transcription, copy	part of the body, document, words	4b13.1, 1093, 3824
V20	騰	TŌ	price rise	part of the body, document, horse	4b16.3, 1106, 3834
V21	実	mino(ru), mi, JITSU	bear fruit, fruit, reality	house, (fact)	3m5.4, 2225, 1297

V21	春	haru, SHUN	spring	fact, sun	4c5.13, 2576, 2122
V21	泰	TAI	tranquil	fact, water	3a5.34, 2583, 2526
V21	奏	kana(deru), SŌ	play music	fact, heaven	0a9.17, 2577, 1178
V21	奉	tatematsu(ru), HŌ	offer respectfully, *dedicate*	fact, two, halve	0a8.13, 2559, 212
V21	俸	HŌ	salary	human being, dedicate	2a8.18, 114, 480
V21	棒	BŌ	rod	wood, dedicate	4a8.20, 983, 2302
V22	邦	HŌ	state, Japan	long life, city wall	2d4.7, 847, 4758
V22	寿	kotobuki, JU	*longevity*	long life, a bit of	0a7.15, 3557, 194
V22	鋳	i(ru), CHŪ	cast	metal, longevity	8a7.2, 1729, 4865
W1	式	SHIKI	style, ceremony	ritual, handicraft	4n3.2, 3049, 1556
W1	試	kokoro(miru), tame(su), SHI	try	words, ritual, handicraft	7a6.18, 1525, 4361

W2	弐	NI	two	lance, two	4n3.3, 3195, 32
W2	武	BU, MU	*military*	lance, stop	4n5.3, 3210, 51
W2	賦	FU	payment, installment	money, military	7b8.4, 1583, 4513
W3	代	ka(waru/eru), DAI, TAI	substitute, generation	grapheme	2a3.3, 30, 364
W3	袋	fukuro, TAI	bag	substitute, clothes	5e5.11, 2588, 4223
W3	貸	ka(su), TAI	lend	substitute, money	7b5.9, 2600, 4503
W4	伐	BATSU	*fell*, log	human being, weapon	2a4.5, 42, 370
W4	閥	BATSU	clique	gate, fell	8e6.2, 3325, 4954
W4	戦	tataka(u), ikusa, SEN	fight, war	single, weapon	4n9.2, 1787, 1810
W4	戯	tawamu(reru), GI	play, jest	tiger, line up, weapon	4n11.1, 1875, 246
W4	賊	ZOKU	bandit	money, weapon, ten	7b6.3, 1530, 4508

W4	戒	imashi(meru), KAI	*warn*, commandment	weapon, flexible	4n3.1, 3204, 1801
W4	械	KAI	simple machine	wood, warn	4a7.22, 961, 2264
W4	幾	iku, KI	*how many*, some	fiber, fiber, weapon, human being	4n8.4, 3582, 1496
W4	機	KI	complicated machine, opportunity	wood, how many	4a12.1, 1076, 2379
W4	域	IKI	bounded area	earth, weapon, mouth, one	3b8.3, 465, 1085
W4	惑	mado(u), WAKU	be perplexed	weapon, mouth, one, heart	4k8.16, 2786, 1710
W5	裁	saba(ku), ta(tsu), SAI	judge, cut clothes	injure, clothes	5e6.9, 3299, 788
W5	栽	SAI	cultivate plants	injure, tree	4n6.1, 3297, 781
W5	載	no(ru/seru), SAI	put in print	injure, vehicle	7c6.5, 3300, 789
W5	纖	SEN	fiber, fine	thread, injure, (line up)	6a11.1, 1413, 3607
W6	識	SHIKI	consciousness, discrimination	words, weaving loom	7a12.6, 1639, 4438

W6	織	o(ru), SHOKU, SHIKI	weave	thread, weaving loom	6a12.6, 1422, 3613
W6	職	SHOKU	employment	ear, weaving loom	6e12.1, 1425, 3718
W7	我	ware, GA	I, one's own	grapheme	0a7.10, 3548, 200
W7	餓	GA	be hungry	eat, one's own	8b7.1, 1734, 5171
W8	義	GI	righteousness, artificial, in-law	grapheme	2o11.3, 2338, 3668
W8	儀	GI	ceremony	human being, righteousness	2a13.4, 169, 554
W8	議	GI	consultation, consideration	words, righteousness	7a13.4, 1647, 4448
W8	犠	GI	sacrifice	cattle, righteousness	4g13.1, 1089, 2865
W9	茂	shige(ru), MO	grow thick	flower, grow	3k5.7, 2245, 3915
W9	越	ko(su), ko(eru), ETSU	surpass, go beyond	run, (grow)	4n8.2, 3314, 4542
W10	歳	SAI	year, age suffix	stop, rear cover, small	4n9.5, 2490, 2434

W10	威	I	authority	rear cover, woman	4n5.2, 3578, 1803
W10	滅	horo(biru/bosu), METSU	be ruined, ruin	water, rear cover, fire	3a10.26, 660, 2660
W10	減	he(ru/rasu), GEN	decrease	water, rear cover, mouth	3a9.37, 601, 2637
W10	感	KAN	*sensation*, feeling	rear cover, mouth, heart	4k9.21, 2835, 1731
W10	憾	KAN	regret	feeling, sensation	4k13.3, 764, 1778
W11	成	na(ru/su), SEI	become, achieve	grapheme	4n2.1, 3537, 1799
W11	盛	saka(ru), mo(ru), SEI	prosper, fill	become, plate	5h6.1, 2675, 3116
W11	誠	makoto, SEI	sincerity	words, become	7a6.3, 1523, 4352
W11	城	shiro, JŌ	castle	earth, become	3b6.1, 352, 1078
W12	浅	asa(i), SEN	shallow	water, superficial	3a6.4, 389, 2549
W12	践	SEN	practical	foot, superficial	7d6.1, 1535, 4558

W12	銭	zeni, SEN	money, one- hundredth of a yen	metal, superficial	8a6.1, 1725, 4851
W12	桟	SAN	plank bridge	wood, superficial	4a6.1, 932, 2252
W12	残	noko(ru/su), ZAN	remain (vi), leave behind (vt)	death, superficial	0a10.11, 943, 2445
X1	当	a(taru/teru), TŌ	hit, prove right, the present	small, broom	3n3.3, 2177, 1359
X1	雪	yuki, SETSU	snow	rain, broom	8d3.2, 2759, 5044
X1	急	iso(gu), KYŪ	hurry	tied up, broom, heart	2n7.2, 2092, 1667
X1	尋	tazu(neru), JIN	inquire	broom, handicraft, mouth, a bit of	3d9.29, 2322, 1585
X1	隠	kaku(reru/su), IN	hide (vi, vt)	fortress, caress, broom, heart	2d11.3, 713, 5020
X1	穏	oda(yaka), ON	calm, mild	rice seedling, caress, broom, heart	5d11.4, 1235, 3305
X2	濯	TAKU	rinse	water, interval	3a14.5, 793, 2718
X2	躍	odo(ru), YAKU	leap, jump	foot, interval	7d7.2, 1658, 4595

X2	曜	YŌ	day of the week	sun, interval	4c14.1, 1096, 2162
X3	侵	oka(su), SHIN	invade	human being, douse	2a7.15, 101, 452
X3	浸	hita(ru/su), SHIN	be soaked in (vi), soak (vt)	water, douse	3a7.17, 442, 2572
X3	寝	ne(ru/kasu), SHIN	go to sleep, put to sleep	house, bed, douse	3m10.1, 2329, 1326
X4	掃	ha(ku), SŌ	sweep	hand, cleanse	3c8.22, 503, 1945
X4	婦	FU	housewife	woman, cleanse	3e8.6, 469, 1237
X5	録	ROKU	record	metal, copper	8a8.16, 1742, 4879
X5	緑	midori, RYOKU	green	thread, copper	6a8.15, 1377, 3564
X5	縁	fuchi, EN	edge, relation	thread, (broom), pork belly	6a9.10, 1386, 3585
X6	唐	kara, TŌ	*Tang Dynasty*	building, broomstick, mouth	3q7.3, 3115, 1516
X6	糖	TŌ	sugar	rice, Tang Dynasty	6b10.3, 1403, 3485

X6	庸	YŌ	mediocre	building, (broomstick), moon	3q8.2, 3128, 1520
X6	妻	tsuma, SAI	wife	one, broomstick, woman	3e5.10, 2558, 1206
X7	粛	SHUKU	purge, solemnly	(sin), one, halve, halve	0a11.8, 3581, 115
X7	康	KŌ	healthy	building, sin	3q8.1, 3124, 1518
X7	逮	TAI	chase	sin, traveler	2q8.2, 3123, 4706
X7	隷	REI	slave	scholar, show, sin	4e11.1, 1751, 5026
X8	津	tsu, SHIN	tidal wave	water, paintbrush	3a6.1, 390, 2543
X8	律	RITSU	law, rhythm	step, paintbrush	3i6.1, 363, 1608
X8	筆	fude, HITSU	writing brush	bamboo, paintbrush	6f6.1, 2677, 3397
X8	建	ta(tsu/teru), KEN	be built (vi), *build* (vt)	paintbrush, big step	2q6.2, 3090, 1549
X8	健	suko(yaka), KEN	robust, healthily	human being, build	2a8.34, 134, 512

X8	書	ka(ku), SHO	write	(paintbrush), sun	4c6.6, 2658, 3719
X8	事	koto, JI	affair, abstract thing	one, mouth, (paintbrush)	0a8.15, 3567, 272
X9	兼	ka(neru), KEN	concurrently, incompetence	grapheme	2o8.1, 2286, 598
X9	嫌	kira(u), KEN	dislike	woman, concurrently	3e10.7, 636, 1250
X9	謙	KEN	humble	words, concurrently	7a10.10, 1617, 4422
X9	廉	REN	incorrupt, cheap	building, concurrently	3q10.1, 3153, 1530
X10	君	kimi, KUN	you, familiar title	grapheme	3d4.23, 3206, 899
X10	郡	GUN	county	you, city wall	2d7.12, 1466, 4764
X10	群	mu(reru), mu(re), GUN	crowd together, group, flock	you, sheep	3d10.14, 1540, 3667
X11	争	araso(u), SŌ	contend	grapheme	2n4.2, 2030, 186
X11	浄	JŌ	clean	water, contend	3a6.18, 382, 2548

X11	静	shizu(maru/meru), shizu(ka), SEI	become quiet (vi), make quiet (vt)	blue, contend	4b10.9, 1728, 5077
Y1	匠	SHŌ	craftsman	box, ax	2t4.2, 2990, 761
Y1	医	I	medicine	box, arrow	2t5.2, 2993, 763
Y1	匿	TOKU	shelter, shield, hide	box, young	2t8.2, 3011, 764
Y1	虐	shiita(geru), GYAKU	tyrannize, treat cruelly	tiger, box, one	2m7.3, 3218, 4106
Y2	区	KU	ward, division	grapheme	2t2.1, 2963, 757
Y2	駆	ka(keru), KU	gallop, drive	horse, division	10a4.5, 1823, 5200
Y2	枢	SŪ	pivot	wood, division	4a4.22, 865, 2208
Y2	欧	Ō	Europe	division, lack	4j4.2, 887, 2413
Y2	殴	nagu(ru), Ō	beat	division, strike	2t6.1, 886, 2451
Y3	匹	hiki, HITSU	counter for animals, comparable	grapheme	2t2.3, 2962, 756

Y3	甚	hanahada(shii), JIN	*extremely*	(game), (comparable)	0a9.10, 2643, 111
Y3	堪	ta(eru), KAN	endure	earth, extremely	3b9.1, 559, 1112
Y3	勘	KAN	perception, intuition	extremely, power	2g9.3, 1777, 729
Y4	巨	KYO	huge	grapheme	2t2.2, 3039, 758
Y4	拒	koba(mu), KYO	refuse, veto	hand, huge	3c5.29, 311, 1847
Y4	距	KYO	distance	foot, huge	7d5.8, 1511, 4548
Y5	臣	SHIN, JIN	minister, retainer	grapheme	2t4.3, 3068, 3837
Y5	姫	hime	princess	woman, minister	3e7.11, 407, 1216
Y5	臨	nozo(mu), RIN	be present	minister, human, article	2t15.1, 1630, 3840
Y5	蔵	kura, ZŌ	*repository*	flower, grow, minister	3k12.17, 2364, 4042
Y5	臓	ZŌ	internal organ	part of the body, repository	4b15.2, 1102, 3828

Y6	覧	RAN	look over	oversee, see	5c12.7, 2854, 4292
Y6	監	KAN	watch over, *supervise*	oversee, plate	5h10.1, 2852, 3121
Y6	艦	KAN	warship	ship, supervise	6c15.2, 1435, 3881
Y6	鑑	KAN	mirror, appraise	metal, supervise	8a15.2, 1773, 4924
Y6	濫	RAN	overflow, excessive	water, supervise	3a15.3, 801, 2724
Y7	堅	kata(i), KEN	firm, solid	massive, earth	3b9.13, 2823, 1096
Y7	賢	kashiko(i), KEN	wise	massive, money	7b9.2, 2839, 4517
Y7	緊	KIN	tight	massive, thread	6a9.17, 2838, 3560
Y8	馬	uma, BA	horse	grapheme	10a0.1, 3296, 5191
Y8	篤	TOKU	serious, cordial	bamboo, horse	6f10.1, 2716, 3434
Y8	驚	odoro(ku/kasu), KYŌ	be surprised (vi), surprise (vt)	respect, horse	10a12.4, 2894, 5229

Y9	己	onore, KO, KI	ego	grapheme	0a3.12, 3380, 1462
Y9	忌	i(mu), i(mawashii), KI	abhor, detestable	ego, heart	4k3.4, 2207, 1463
Y9	記	shiru(su), KI	write down	words, ego	7a3.5, 1453, 4318
Y9	紀	KI	report	thread, ego	6a3.5, 1276, 3497
Y9	起	o(kiru/kosu), o(koru), KI	get up, wake someone up, occur	run, ego	3b7.11, 3307, 4541
Y9	妃	HI	princess	woman, ego	3e3.2, 206, 1188
Y9	配	kuba(ru), HAI	distribute	wine, ego	7e3.2, 1460, 4779
Y9	改	arata(maru/meru), KAI	be renewed (vi), reform (vt)	ego, teacher	4i3.1, 243, 1464
Y9	巻	ma(ku), maki, KAN	*roll up*, volume	document, ego	0a9.11, 2645, 1466
Y9	圏	KEN	sphere	enclosed, roll up	3s9.1, 3148, 1045
Y9	港	minato, KŌ	harbor	water, joint, ego	3a9.13, 605, 2630

Y9	遷	SEN	transfer	west, big, ego, traveler	2q12.1, 3170, 4743
Y9	選	era(bu), SEN	choose	ego, ego, joint, traveler	2q12.3, 3169, 4744
Y10	包	tsutsu(mu), HŌ	wrap, encompass	grapheme	0a5.9, 2966, 176
Y10	泡	awa, HŌ	bubble	water, wrap	0a5.18, 334, 2523
Y10	抱	da(ku), kaka(eru), HŌ	hug, hold in the arms	hand, wrap	3c5.15, 306, 1883
Y10	胞	HŌ	cell, membranous sac	part of the body, wrap	4b5.5, 917, 3749
Y10	砲	HŌ	heavy gun, cannon	stone, wrap	5a5.3, 1151, 3185
Y10	飽	a(kiru/kasu), HŌ	be satiated, surfeit	eat, wrap	8b5.1, 1715, 5162
Y11	弓	yumi, KYŪ	bow	grapheme	3h0.1, 3383, 1560
Y11	引	hi(keru/ku), IN	draw, pull	bow, halve	3h1.1, 181, 1562
Y11	湾	WAN	bay	water, pink, bow	3a9.15, 613, 2627

Y11	弱	yowa(ru), yowa(i), JAKU	weaken, weak	bow, ice, bow, ice	3h7.2, 1167, 650
Y12	弔	tomura(u), CHŌ	condolence, mourn	grapheme	0a4.41, 3432, 80
Y12	弟	otōto, TEI	younger brother	(horns), condolence, drop	2o5.1, 2044, 584
Y12	第	DAI	ordinal number prefix	bamboo, condolence, drop	6f5.5, 2660, 3385
Y13	沸	wa(ku/kasu), FUTSU	boil (vi/vt)	water, cook up	3a5.3, 329, 2524
Y13	費	tsui(yasu), HI	spend	cook up, money	7b5.4, 2607, 4497
Y14	巧	taku(mi), KŌ	skillful	handicraft, dirty	0a5.7, 188, 1453
Y14	朽	ku(chiru), KYŪ	decay	tree, dirty	4a2.6, 821, 2175
Y14	極	kiwa(maru/meru), KYOKU	reach an extreme pole	tree, (dirty), mouth, moreover, one	4a8.11, 1017, 2305
Y14	号	GŌ	number	mouth, dirty	3d2.10, 2135, 882
Y14	誇	hoko(ru), KO	boast	words, big, one, dirty	7a6.9, 1522, 4354

Y14	汚	yogo(reru/su), kitana(i), O	become dirty (vi), defile (vt)	water, one, dirty	3a3.5, 222, 2494
Y15	考	kanga(eru), KŌ	think	grapheme	2k4.4, 3196, 3684
Y15	拷	GŌ	torture	hand, think	3c6.2, 373, 1895
Y15	襲	oso(u), SHŪ	attack	stand, part of the body, ..., clothes	5e16.2, 2917, 5443
Y16	与	ata(eru), YO	give, impart	grapheme	0a3.23, 3421, 6
Y16	写	utsu(ru/su), SHA	take a picture (vt), copy	cover, give	2i3.1, 2000, 626
Y17	呉	GO	kingdom of Wu (China)	grapheme	2o5.7, 2549, 583
Y17	娯	GO	enjoyment	woman, kingdom of Wu	3e7.3, 405, 1226
Y17	誤	ayama(ru), GO	be mistaken	words, kingdom of Wu	7a7.2, 1542, 4372
Y17	虞	osore	fear	tiger, kingdom of Wu	2m11.1, 3254, 4110
Z1	直	nao(ru/su), CHOKU, JIKI	be fixed (vi), *fix* (vt), straight	ten, eye, corner	2k6.2, 2932, 775

Z1	置	o(ku), CHI, SHI	place, put	net, fix	5g8.8, 2608, 3644
Z1	値	ne, atai, CHI	value	human being, fix	2a8.30, 109, 488
Z1	植	u(waru/eru), SHOKU	be planted, plant	tree, fix	4a8.32, 990, 2303
Z1	殖	fu(eru/yasu), SHOKU	multiply	death, fix	5c7.4, 994, 2448
Z1	断	kotowa(ru), ta(tsu), DAN	decline, cut off, decision	rice, corner, ax	6b5.6, 1492, 2078
Z1	継	tsu(gu), KEI	succeed	thread, corner, rice	6a7.8, 1360, 3545
Z1	県	KEN	*prefecture*	eye, corner, small	3n6.3, 2641, 1362
Z1	懸	ka(karu/keru), KEN	hang, suspend	prefecture, lineage, heart	4k16.2, 2915, 1790
Z2	印	shirushi, IN	mark, seal	rank, seal	2e4.1, 828, 102
Z2	潟	kata	beach	water, (rank), (rank), envelope, cooking fire	3a12.9, 745, 2695
Z2	興	oko(ru/su), KŌ, KYŌ	prosper, revive, interest	(rank), same, (rank), stool	2o14.2, 2909, 615

Z2	段	DAN	*stairs*	(rank), drop, strike	2s7.2, 1144, 2452
Z2	鍛	kita(eru), TAN	forge, train	metal, stairs	8a9.5, 1755, 4895
Z2	暇	hima, KA	free time	sun, ... , moreover	4c9.1, 1012, 2152
Z3	非	HI	is not, negative assessment	grapheme	0a8.1, 889, 5080
Z3	悲	kana(shimu), kana(shii), HI	feel sad, sad	negative assessment, heart	4k8.18, 2775, 5082
Z3	扉	tobira, HI	hinged door	door, negative assessment	4m8.2, 1955, 1825
Z3	俳	HAI	actor, haiku	human being, negative assessment	2a8.8, 112, 485
Z3	排	HAI	exclude, expel	hand, negative assessment	3c5.3, 490, 1884
Z3	輩	HAI	fellow	negative assessment, vehicle	7c8.7, 2807, 5086
Z3	罪	tsumi, ZAI	crime	net, negative assessment	5g8.4, 2610, 3643
Z4	不	FU, BU	not, negation of condition	grapheme	0a4.2, 3434, 17

Z4	否	ina, HI	denial	negation of condition, mouth	3d4.20, 2406, 40
Z4	杯	sakazuki, HAI	wine glass, cup	wood, negation of condition	4a4.11, 857, 2206
Z5	無	na(i), MU, BU	without, negation of existence	negation of existence, cooking fire	4d8.8, 2135, 2773
Z5	舞	ma(u), BU	dance	negation of existence, opposition	0a15.1, 2146, 3862
Z6	片	kata, HEN	one-sided	grapheme	2j2.5, 3461, 2842
Z6	版	HAN	printing plate, publishing	one-sided, against	2j6.8, 872, 2843
Z7	后	KŌ	empress	circulation, one, mouth	3d3.11, 2981, 181
Z7	盾	tate, JUN	*shield*	circulation, ten, eye	5c4.8, 3006, 215
Z7	循	JUN	circulate	step, shield	3i9.6, 578, 1625
Z7	逓	TEI	relay	circulation, two, cloth, traveler	2q7.5, 3106, 4695
Z7	派	HA	sect, dispatch	water, circulation, (far)	3a6.21, 381, 2547

Z7	脈	MYAKU	vein, pulse	part of the body, circulation, (far)	4b6.8, 953, 3764
Z7	孤	KO	solitary	child, circulation, (oneself), drop	2c6.2, 356, 1270
Z7	弧	KO	arc	bow, circulation, (oneself), drop	3h6.2, 360, 1567
Z8	秀	hii(deru), SHŪ	*excel*	rice seedling, spectacular	5d2.4, 2545, 3263
Z8	透	su(ku/kasu), TŌ	transparent	excel, traveler	2q7.10, 3108, 4699
Z8	誘	saso(u), YŪ	invite, induce	words, excel	7a7.4, 1550, 4371
Z8	携	tazusa(waru), KEI	participate in, carry in hand	hand, chicken, spectacular	3c10.4, 648, 1977
Z9	及	oyo(bu), KYŪ	reach to, as well as	grapheme	0a3.24, 3385, 154
Z9	吸	su(u), KYŪ	breathe in, suck	mouth, reach to	3d3.5, 202, 885
Z9	級	KYŪ	grade	thread, reach to	6a3.2, 1279, 3496
Z9	扱	atsuka(u)	handle	hand, reach to	3c3.5, 217, 1836

Z10	幻	maboroshi, GEN	vision, illusion	fiber, take care	0a4.6, 180, 1494
Z10	局	KYOKU	bureau, limited part	behind, take care, mouth	3r4.4, 3063, 1384
Z10	司	SHI	*administer*	take care, one, mouth	3d2.14, 2931, 877
Z10	伺	ukaga(u), SHI	(humble) inquire	human being, administer	2a5.23, 69, 395
Z10	詞	SHI	words	words, administer	7a5.15, 1503, 4335
Z10	飼	ka(u), SHI	raise animals	eat, administer	8b5.4, 1716, 5163
Z10	嗣	SHI	heir	mouth, (counter for books), administer	3d10.13, 1719, 969
Z11	乏	tobo(shii), BŌ	insufficient	drop, too little	0a3.11, 1933, 150
Z11	芝	shiba	lawn, turf	flower, too little	3k2.1, 2180, 3893
Z12	為	I	do for the sake of	grapheme	4d5.8, 3577, 138
Z12	偽	itsuwa(ru), nise, GI	lie, cheat	human being, do for the sake of	2a9.2, 131, 510

Z13	入	hai(ru), i(reru), NYŪ	enter (vi), put in (vt)	grapheme	0a2.3, 3370, 574
Z13	込	ko(mu/meru)	move inward, be crowded	enter, traveler	2q2.3, 3030, 4660
Z14	逆	saka(rau), GYAKU	reverse	face to face, traveler	2q6.8, 3091, 4685
Z14	塑	SO	model, mold	face to face, moon, earth	3b10.8, 2843, 1121
Z15	敢	KAN	brave	grapheme	4i8.5, 1706, 2054
Z15	厳	kibi(shii), GEN	strict, severe	gather, cliff, brave	3n14.1, 3289, 253
Z16	身	mi, SHIN	body, one's person	grapheme	0a7.5, 3553, 4601
Z16	射	i(ru), SHA	*shoot*	body, a bit of	0a10.8, 1458, 4603
Z16	謝	ayama(ru), SHA	apologize	words, shoot	7a10.1, 1620, 4423
Z16	窮	kiwa(maru/meru), KYŪ	end, finish	airhole, body, bow	3m12.4, 2358, 3337
Z17	慶	KEI	congratulate	pretty, (one), heart, march	3q12.8, 3173, 1539

Z17	薦	susu(meru), SEN	recommend	flower, pretty, dirty, cooking fire	3k13.25, 2373, 4067
Z17	麗	uruwa(shii), REI	pretty	..., pretty, compare	3q16.5, 2151, 5381
Z18	帰	kae(ru/su), KI	return (vi), dismiss (vt)	long sword, cleanse	2f8.8, 130, 1582
Z18	班	HAN	corps, squad	king, long sword, king	4f6.3, 946, 2935
Z19	幣	HEI	paper offerings	bank note, cloth	3f12.4, 2885, 1490
Z19	弊	HEI	evil, abuse	bank note, flexible	4i11.3, 2884, 1551
Z20	隔	heda(taru/teru), KAKU	be apart (vi), separate (vt)	fortress, ditch	2d10.2, 671, 5016
Z20	融	YŪ	melt	ditch, insect	6d10.5, 1831, 5274
Z21	世	yo, SEI, SE	world, age	grapheme	0a5.37, 3496, 95
Z21	葉	ha, YŌ	leaf	flower, the world, tree	3k9.21, 2321, 4001
Z21	華	hana, KA	flower, China	flower, ...	3k7.1, 2283, 3955

Z22	憂	ure(eru), ure(i), YŪ	*be anxious*	troubled, heart, march	4i12.1, 2145, 70
Z22	優	sugu(reru), yasa(shii), YŪ	excel, gentle	human being, be anxious	2a15.1, 177, 564
Z22	寡	KA	alone	house, (troubled), stool, sword	3m11.2, 2344, 1337
Z23	修	osa(maru/meru), SHŪ	govern oneself, master	human being, halve, teacher, style	2a8.11, 123, 491
Z23	面	omote, tsura, MEN	face	one, drop, enclosed, ...	3s6.1, 2087, 5087
Z23	互	taga(i), GO	reciprocal	...	0a4.15, 3437, 14
Z23	瓶	BIN	bottle	(horns), with both hands, ...	2o9.6, 1344, 2984
Z23	繭	mayu, KEN	cocoon	flower, cavity, halve, thread, insect	3k15.7, 2380, 4087
Z23	璽	JI	imperial seal	one, animal legs, cavity, halve, (4x)scissors, gem	4f14.2, 2911, 71
Z23	凸	TOTSU	convex	...	0a5.13, 3486, 90
Z23	凹	Ō	concave	...	0a5.14, 3482, 664

Grapheme Index

a bit of	E10
a certain	K7
ability	Q3
act violently	P3
add	B4
additionally	C15
administer	Z10
again	L20
against	R9
airhole	N5
all	N11
alms	D7
already	N8
altar	LE12
ambition	I1
an official	V7
angle	L18
angle of 90°	N21
animal legs	BO1
appearance	T17
army	L5
arrival	Q6
arrive	Q6
arrow	H7
article	B1
as	V11
ash	A7
Asia	I11
attach	E11
augment	D5
autumn	A7
ax	A20
bamboo	TO7
bamboo	H11
bank note	Z19
barn	T6
barracks	N18
barrier	F12
basis	J6
be anxious	Z22
be in between	T3
be wild	M5
bean	B6
bear	A10
beard	L12
become	W11
bed	LE4
behind	U1
belong to	U1
belt	L1
bend	D8
better	I19
big	FR7
big	V9
big step	EN5
bird	C11
bird's nest	J3
black	D12
blade	A10
bless	D7
block of houses	E1
blood	A14
blue	I15
boar	S13
body	Z16
bone	L10
both	L6
bottle	G13
bow	LE9
bow	Y11
box	Y1
branch	R10
brave	Z15
break	A20
breath	C16
bright	B5
broom	X1
broomstick	X6
bucket	F2
Buddhist temple	E12
build	X8
building	EN2
bundle	J11
can	H8
cap	M1
capital	M3
caress	TO10
cattle	H1
cause	V9
cavity	L6
center	V18
central point	B15
change into	N10
chapter	M14
characteristic	N23
chastity	C19
check	T11
chicken	RI7
chicken	G14
chief	B9
child	A15
choice	V17
circle	L18
circulation	Z7
city wall	RI3
cleanse	X4
cliff	EN1
climb	T1
cloth	FR5
clothes	P7
cloud	Q5
command	T8
common	L24
comparable	Y3
compare	N11
completion	N6
complicated	P6
comrade	D9
concealed	V10
concurrently	X9
condolence	Y12
constant	O6
container	A19
contend	X11
conversion	T12
cook up	Y13
cooking fire	BO4
copper	X5
corner	Z1
correct	O5
counsel	M19
counter for books	L19
countryside	D12
court	G7
cover	L1

crouch N9
cultivate I13
cut N15
dance O7
danger L10
death S20
deceased M5
dedicate V21
degree R1
demand L12
descendants N11
despise F2
determine O6
development Q8
devil Q11
die S20
different K12
difficult V16
direction M6
dirty Y14
ditch Z20
divine B3
divining rod FR4
division Y2
do for the sake of Z12
document V20
dog V11
door U4
doubt O7
douse X3
dragon N19
drop FR1
dry F7
dry up S7
duty G6
each S26
eagle H9
ear A6
earlier H3
early F5
earth FR6
earth I3
east J12
easy S8
eat LE20
eat T7
ego Y9
eight T14
elite L3
emperor M18
employ someone U4
empty N5
enclosed EN6
enjoy M2
enlarge U5
enter Z13
envelope S3
equal M8
escape from S2
eternal P2
evening S17
every A16
evil A19
excel Z8
exclusive E13
expanse E8
expel A20
extend O3
extremely Y3
eye C13
face to face Z14
fact V21
fair O10
family P11
far P4
farming P10
father A17
feather A22
feeling LE3
fell W4
festival R5
feudal lord H7
fiber Q13
filial piety I6
fill Q10
finish E2
fire A7
first in a series D10
first time M16
fish D4
fishing rod L17
fit T10
five I9
fix Z1
flame A7
flat F9
flesh L7
flexible K3
flower TO6
fog F6
fold S24
follow O6
foot LE18
forest J4
former C4
former times K11
fortress LE8
friend V6
from heaven V14
fruit D14
fun C5
game K8
gate C8
gather TO9
gem I17
general officer E10
generate H10
give Y16
go G12
go away Q7
go out A4
good C10
good luck I2
government B10
grief P5
group of people M12
grow W9
grow late V8
guest S26
hair N17
halberd E3
half F11
halve FR3
hand G8
hand LE11

handicraft	I8	inspect	R5	make efforts	E3
hang down	G10	intermingle	M9	male name suffix	C10
happiness	F7	intermittent	C8	man	D1
hard	F4	interval	X2	management	B11
harm	I13	intimate	S14	manifold	K4
harvest	J2	Japanese restaurant	M2	many	S17
have	V2	joint	K12	march	S23
head	RI6	kernel	Q12	market	M4
heap of earth	I5	king	I17	massive	Y7
heart	BO3	king	LE15	master	I18
heart	N3	kingdom of Wu	Y17	measure	U3
heat	S10	know	H7	meet	T2
heaven	V13	lack	S15	member	C19
heavy	G3	lambswool	I19	metal	LE21
hemp	J5	lance	W2	metal	T5
herbs	K10	last part	J8	middle	B12
hermit	A4	lean over	U1	middle course	B14
high	M2	leather	K4	military	W2
hill	A21	leave over	T4	minister	Y5
history	V7	left	V5	money	C19
home	S12	legs	BO2	moon	RI8
hometown	Q13	let go	M6	moon	L14
honor	N7	levy	I17	moreover	R1
hook	N1	lieutenant	U1	morning	F6
horns	TO1	life	H4	most	R2
horse	LE22	light	A1	mother	A16
horse	Y8	lightning	N19	mountain	A4
hot	M17	line up	I10	mourning	P8
house	TO5	lineage	Q17	mouth	B1
how many	W4	linen	V3	move	G3
huge	Y4	little	A13	mutual	C14
human	TO11	little child	M11	name	S19
human being	A3	livestock	Q15	neck	C17
human being	LE5	lodge	C7	negation of condition	Z4
hundred	C7	logic	T13	negation of existence	Z5
husband	V15	long	P9	negative assessment	Z3
ice	LE1	long duration	S22	net	TO8
immediate	C9	long life	V22	never	S8
in general	R6	long sword	Z18	next	S16
in advance	E2	longevity	V22	night	S23
increase	P14	lose	H6	nine	N20
inferior	I14	low	P12	noble	C19
injure	W5	lower	A1	noon	H8
insect	B13	lust	N24	north	N12
inside	L7	maintenance	Q16	nose	C16

nosegay	K1	prize	L3	righteousness	W8
not yet	J7	profit	G4	rise	A1
notify	H2	profound	Q15	risk	C13
now	T9	prohibition	J4	ritual	W1
number	G5	prominent	F5	river	A8
officer	B10	promise	I13	road	S26
old	F3	prosperity	D3	robe	LE13
older brother	B7	protect	E10	roll up	Y9
one	A1	protector	P16	roof	T2
one's own	W7	province	A8	round	N22
one-sided	Z6	public	T15	row	S21
one of a pair	R4	purport	N13	rule	C20
oneself	Q1	quantity	D12	run	O9
open hole	N1	rain	TO12	run out	T16
opposition	S18	raise	Q9	same	L8
origin	N6	rank	Z2	satan	B8
original	C6	reach to	Z9	scene	M3
outside	P15	reality	V4	scholar	I1
oversee	Y6	rear cover	W10	school house	L2
paintbrush	X8	reason	D6	scissors	A18
part	T14	receive	R1	scoop	S4
part of the body	BO5	recover	V12	scorch	G14
part of the body	LE24	red	I4	scorpion	L13
peaceful	A11	reform	K5	seal	RI4
penalty	K2	religion	E7	second class	N2
penetrate	C19	rely on	J11	see	C18
people	P13	repeat	S24	seedling	D2
period of time	C3	replace	V15	seek	P3
periphery	L9	report	D11	sell	L4
phenomenon	S11	repository	Y5	sensation	W10
phrase	S5	require	I12	seven	N15
pinch	V19	resemble	L15	sheep	F10
pink	M10	reside	U1	shield	Z7
pity	P5	resin	J9	ship	L22
plate	A14	respect	S5	shoot	Z16
platform	Q2	responsibility	I16	show	E7
pork belly	S11	return	U4	sickness	EN3
porter	G6	rice	LE7	sin	X7
possibility	E4	rice	J10	single	D13
power	A9	rice field	D1	sink	N8
prefecture	Z1	rice seedling	LE6	skin	R11
present	I17	rice seedling	G4	slave	R8
preserve	J1	ride	G9	slip	I12
pretty	Z17	ridge of a roof	J12	small	TO2
prison	U2	right	V1	small	A12

small shop	U1
snake	N24
soldier	A21
solid	C9
sound	M13
south	L6
spectacular	Z8
spring	P1
squad	S13
stable	V5
stairs	Z2
stamina	M20
stand	M11
start	T1
steel	L11
step	G11
stimulate	S25
stomach	D1
stone	A5
stool	T18
stop	O1
storehouse	U6
strengthen	Q14
strike	R6
structure	L21
style	RI1
substitute	W3
suffice	O8
summon	B5
sun	LE23
sun	C1
sunrise	C2
superficial	W12
supervise	Y6
surface	P5
sweet	K6
sword	A10
sword	RI2
system	H1
table	L23
take	R2
take care	Z10
talent	E9
Tang dynasty	X6
teacher	RI5
ten	F1
ten-day period	S6
ten thousand	S9
the world	Z21
thick	V9
thief	F13
think	Y15
third class	L7
thousand	G1
thread	Q16
thread	LE14
three	A2
tied up	TO4
tiger	N16
tongue	G2
too little	Z11
tool	T18
tooth	O1
trade	S1
traveler	EN4
treat	S23
tree, wood	LE16
tree, wood	J1
tremble	P10
trillion	N14
troubled	Z22
truth	T18
turn around	B1
tusk	E6
two	A2
typical	TO3
uncle	R3
unusual	E5
urban prefecture	E11
use	L16
valley	T17
vehicle	C12
vermilion	H5
vertical	R7
very much	FR2
vibrate	F8
vigorous	I1
visit a holy place	Q1
volcano	T1
walk	O2
warn	W4
watchdog	LE10
watchtower	M2
water	LE2
water	P1
wave	R11
way	C17
weapon	W4
weaving loom	W6
well	K9
west	I12
what	E4
white	C5
whole	T2
wholesale	O4
wide	Q4
widespread	I10
will	M15
wine	N7
wine	LE19
winter	S23
with both hands	K2
withdraw	Q7
without fail	N4
woman	A11
words	LE17
words	B2
working person	I7
wrap	Y10
wriggle	N25
writings	M7
yellow	K10
you	X10
young	V1

Stroke Count Index

1: 丶FR1 丨FR3 一A1 乚N1 乙N2 𠃊Z1 ㇆Z10

2: 八BO1 儿BO2 刂RI2 卩RI4 𠂉TO11 丷TO3 ⺈TO4 冫LE1 亻LE5 辶EN4
卜FR4 厂EN1 二A2 人A3 力A9 刀A10 乂A18 凵A19 丁E1 了E2 十F1
冖L1 冂L6 几L23 亠M1 七N15 匕N9 九N20 㔾N23 厶Q1 又R1 勹S3
八T14 𠆢T2 𠂇V5 匸Y1 丂Y14 ⺁Z7 乃Z8 入Z13 𠃋Z18

3: 彡RI1 阝RI3 ⺍TO1 ⺌TO2 宀TO5 艹TO6 犭LE10 扌LE11 氵LE2 忄LE3 丬LE4 阝LE8 弓LE9 巾FR5 土FR6 大FR7 广EN2 廴EN5 ⺍OB9 囗EN6 山A4 川A8 女A11 小A12 子A15 口B1 于E8 才E9 寸E10 干F7
千G1 彳G11 士I1 土I3 工I8 廾K3 凡L24 亡M5 尢N8 丸N22 也N25
幺Q13 夕S17 久S22 夂S23 勺S4 万S9 六T18 尸U1 ナV4 大V9 弋W1
彐X1 己Y9 弓Y11 与Y16 及Z9 之Z11

4: 冃BO5 心BO3 灬BO4 攵RI5 月RI8 ⺤TO10 礻LE12 𤣩LE15 木LE16
日LE23 月LE24 乂FR2 火A7 少A13 父A17 斤A20 中B12 日C1 斗F2 丰F12
壬G6 手G8 升G13 牛H1 午H8 五I9 龶I13 王I17 木J1 开K2 廿K4 龷K10
井K9 月L14 円L18 内L4 方M6 文M7 心N3 元N6 化N10 比N11 毛N17 屯N18 卆N21 巴N24 止O1 水P1 氏P11 卬P16 ⺗P4 氺P5 业P8
云Q5 亠Q8 支R10 殳R6 反R9 欠S15 歹S20 勿S8 公T15 介T3 今T9
尺U3 戸U4 犬V11 天V13 夫V15 夬V17 丰V22 友V6 弌W2 戈W4 ⺕X6 弔Y12 区Y2 匹Y3 𠂢Z2 不Z4 片Z6

5: ⺲TO8 衤LE13 禾LE6 疒EN3 石A5 皿A14 母A16 丘A21 占B3
加B4 召B5 兄B7 目B10 𠀎B14 目C13 且C15 旦C2 旧C4 白C5
田D1 由D6 甲D10 申D11 矛E3 可E4 牙E6 示E7 付E11 半F11 古F3
平F9 𥝌G4 生H4 失H6 矢H7 乍H10 主I18 本J6 未J7 末J8 朮J9
冉K1 甘K6 用L16 冊L19 ⺌L2 亠M2 市M4 立M11 必N4 宂N5
北N12 电N19 正O5 疋O6 ⺪O7 氐P12 民P13 以P14 卯P15 永P2
玄Q15 台Q2 広Q4 去Q7 圣R7 奴R8 皮R11 句S5 癶T1 令T8 㕣T16
右V1 布V3 史V7 央V18 𡗗V21 代W3 戊W9 包Y10 弗Y13 巨Y4
世Z21

6: ⺮TO7 糸LE14 米LE7 耳A6 羽A22 自B9 虫B13 亘C3 百C7 艮C9
自C16 𠃛D7 曲D8 寺E12 羊F10 早F5 舌G2 行G12 先H3
朱H5 竹H11 西I12 𦍌I19 吉I2 圭I5 米J10 共K12 同L8 而L12
再L20 舟L22 交M9 亦M10 ⺍M18 冋M19 产M20 旨N13 兆N14 虍N16
衣P7 至Q6 充Q10 亥Q12 𢆶Q14 糸Q16 旬S6 次S16 名S19 列S21
各S26 合T10 有V2 关V14 夹V19 共V20 戋W5 戌W10 成W11 戋W12
争X11 聿X8 考Y15 并Z14

7: 𧾷 LE18 酉 LE19 呂 B11 串 B15 言 B2 豆 B6 兑 B8 良 C10 鳥 C11 車 C12
見 C18 貝 C19 里 D12 廷 G7 告 H2 亜 I11 赤 I4 孝 I6 束 J11 売 L4 肖 L15
甫 L17 訁 LI17 辛 M17 酉 N7 足 O8 走 O9 辰 P10 求 P3 系 Q17 豕 S11
舛 S18 夋 S25 余 T4 谷 T17 更 V8 我 W7 君 X10 㚔 X3 呉 Y17 臣 Y5
身 Z16 严 Z17 釆 G5

8: 隹 RI 7 雨 TO12 飠 LE20 金 LE21 門 C8 果 D14 苗 D2 奇 E5 固 F4 卓 F6
垂 G10 隹 G14 並 I10 青 I15 者 I7 采 J2 林 J4 東 J12 其 K8 昔 K11 周 L9 尚 L3
岡 L11 音 M12 京 M3 斉 M8 歩 O2 延 O3 長 P9 育 Q9 取 R2 叔 R3 免 S2
曷 S7 金 T5 舎 T6 㑒 T11 侖 T13 帚 X4 彔 X5 隶 X7 非 Z3 無 Z5 亞 Z22

9: 頁 RI 6 相 C14 首 C17 則 C20 畐 D3 単 D13 専 E13 䍃 F8 重 G3 乗 G9
革 K5 某 K7 禺 L13 軍 L5 音 M13 亲 M16 卸 O4 是 O10 奐 S1 昜 S10
彖 S13 复 S24 食 T7 俞 T12 扁 U5 臤 Y7 為 Z12 咼 L10

10: 馬 LE22 原 C6 韋 F13 堇 I14 冓 L21 鬼 Q11 能 Q3 隻 R4 家 S12 倉 U6
莫 V10 莫 V16 兼 X9 臥 Y6 馬 Y8 鬲 Z20

11: 魚 D4 曽 D5 曹 D9 隺 H9 責 I16 麻 J5 章 M14 祭 R5

12: 尞 V12 戠 W6 敢 Z15 敝 Z19

13: 喿 J3 意 M15 襄 P6 辟 U2 義 W8 貇 S14

14: 翟 X2

Reading Index

A	亜 I11
aba(ku)	暴 P3
aba(reru)	暴 P3
a(biru/biseru)	浴 T17
abu(nai)	危 N23
abura	脂 N13
abura	油 D6
a(garu/geru)	揚 S10
a(garu/geru)	上 A1
a(garu/geru)	挙 T18
AI	哀 P5
AI	愛 S23
ai	相 C14
aida	間 C8
aji	味 J7
aji(wau)	味 J7
aka	赤 I4
aka(i)	赤 I4
aka(ramu)	赤 I4
aka(rui)	明 L14
aka(rui)	明 L14
akatsuki	暁 K1
aki	秋 A7
akina(u)	商 M19
aki(raka)	明 L14
a(kiru/kasu)	飽 Y10
a(ku/keru)	開 K2
AKU	握 U1
AKU	悪 I11
ama	雨 L6
ama	尼 U1
ama	天 V13
ama(eru/yakasu)	甘 K6
ama(i)	甘 K6
ama(ru/su)	余 T4
ame	雨 L6
ame	天 V13
ami	網 M5
a(mu)	編 U5
AN	安 A11
AN	案 A11
AN	暗 M13
ana	穴 T14
anado(ru)	侮 A16
ane	姉 M4
ani	兄 B7
ao	青 I15
ao(gu)	仰 P16
ao(i)	青 I15
ara(i)	荒 M5
ara(i)	粗 C15
araso(u)	争 X11
ara(ta)	新 M16
arata(maru/meru)	改 Y9
ara(u)	洗 H3
arawa(reru/su)	現 C18
arawa(reru/su)	表 P5
arawa(su)	著 I7
a(reru/rasu)	荒 M5
a(ru)	在 V4
a(ru)	有 V2
aru(ku)	歩 O2
asa	朝 F6
asa	麻 J5
asa(i)	浅 W12
ase	汗 F7
ase(ru)	焦 G14
ashi	足 O8
ashi	脚 Q7
aso(bu)	遊 M6
ata(eru)	与 Y16
atai	値 Z1
atai	価 I12
atama	頭 B6
atara(shii)	新 M16
ata(ri)	辺 A10
a(taru/teru)	当 X1
atata(kai)	温 C1
atata(kai)	暖 V6
atata(maru/meru)	温 C1
atata(maru/meru)	暖 V6
a(teru)	充 Q10
ato	跡 M10
ato	後 S23
ATSU	圧 I3
atsu(i)	厚 C1
atsu(i)	熱 N22
atsu(i)	暑 I7
atsuka(u)	扱 Z9
atsu(maru/meru)	集 G14
a(u/wasu)	合 T10
a(u)	遭 D9
a(u)	会 T2
awa	泡 Y10
awa(i)	淡 A7
awa(remu)	哀 P5
awa(seru)	併 K2
awa(teru)	慌 M5
ayama(ru)	謝 Z16
ayama(ru)	誤 Y17
aya(shii)	怪 R7
aya(shimu)	怪 R7
ayatsu(ru)	操 J3
aya(ui)	危 N23
ayu(mu)	歩 O2
aza	字 A15
azamu(ku)	欺 S15
aza(yaka)	鮮 F10
azu(karu/keru)	預 E2
BA	婆 R11
BA	馬 Y8
ba	場 S10
BACHI	罰 B2
BAI	賠 M12
BAI	梅 A16
BAI	倍 M12
BAI	媒 K7

BAI	買 C19	BO	墓 V10	BU	歩 O2
BAI	陪 M12	BO	母 A16	BU	武 W2
BAI	売 L4	BO	簿 E13	BU	分 T14
BAI	培 M12	BO	募 V10	BU	舞 Z5
ba(keru/kasu)	化 N10	BO	慕 V10	BU	部 M12
BAKU	爆 P3	BO	暮 V10	BU	侮 A16
BAKU	麦 S23	BO	模 V10	BU	不 Z4
BAKU	幕 V10	BŌ	剖 M12	BUN	文 M7
BAKU	漠 V10	BŌ	某 K7	BUN	聞 C8
BAKU	縛 E13	BŌ	坊 M6	BUN	分 T14
BAN	蛮 M10	BŌ	棒 V21	buta	豚 S11
BAN	板 R9	BŌ	貿 P15	BUTSU	物 S8
BAN	伴 F11	BŌ	帽 C13	BUTSU	仏 Q1
BAN	万 S9	BŌ	妄 M5	BYAKU	白 C5
BAN	判 F11	BŌ	暴 P3	BYŌ	描 D2
BAN	晩 S2	BŌ	肪 M6	BYŌ	猫 D2
BAN	盤 R6	BŌ	傍 M18	BYŌ	病 L7
BAN	番 G5	BŌ	妨 M6	BYŌ	平 F9
BATSU	末 J8	BŌ	紡 M6	BYŌ	苗 D2
BATSU	閥 W4	BŌ	忘 M5	BYŌ	秒 A13
BATSU	伐 W4	BŌ	冒 C13	CHA	茶 T2
BATSU	罰 B2	BŌ	謀 K7	CHAKU	嫡 M19
BATSU	抜 V6	BŌ	乏 Z11	CHAKU	着 I19
be	辺 A10	BŌ	膨 I2	CHI	致 Q6
BEI	米 J10	BŌ	忙 M5	CHI	治 Q2
BEN	便 V8	BŌ	房 U4	CHI	痴 H7
BEN	勉 S2	BŌ	望 M5	CHI	恥 A6
BEN	弁 Q1	BŌ	亡 M5	CHI	地 N25
beni	紅 I8	BŌ	防 M6	CHI	稚 G14
BETSU	別 S9	BOKU	撲 V15	CHI	置 Z1
BI	備 L16	BOKU	朴 J1	CHI	知 H7
BI	尾 U1	BOKU	僕 V15	CHI	池 N25
BI	美 I19	BOKU	木 J1	CHI	値 Z1
BI	微 N6	BOKU	墨 D12	CHI	遅 U1
BI	鼻 K3	BOKU	牧 H1	chi	血 A14
BIN	敏 A16	BON	盆 T14	chi	乳 N1
BIN	貧 T14	BON	凡 L24	chi	千 G1
BIN	瓶 Z23	BOTSU	没 R6	chichi	乳 N1
BIN	便 V8	BU	無 Z5	chichi	父 A17

chiga(u)	違 F13
chigi(ru)	契 I13
chii(sai)	小 A12
chiji(maru/meru)	縮 C7
chiji(reru/rasu)	縮 C7
chika(i)	近 A20
chikara	力 A9
chika(u)	誓 B2
CHIKU	畜 Q15
CHIKU	蓄 Q15
CHIKU	築 L24
CHIKU	竹 H11
CHIKU	逐 S11
CHIN	沈 N8
CHIN	朕 V14
CHIN	陳 J12
CHIN	鎮 T18
CHIN	珍 T2
CHIN	賃 G6
chi(ru/rasu)	散 K10
CHITSU	窒 Q6
CHITSU	秩 H6
CHO	著 I7
CHO	貯 E1
CHO	緒 I7
CHŌ	帳 P9
CHŌ	脹 P9
CHŌ	庁 E1
CHŌ	眺 N14
CHŌ	長 P9
CHŌ	重 G3
CHŌ	頂 E1
CHŌ	懲 I17
CHŌ	弔 Y12
CHŌ	兆 N14
CHŌ	徴 I17
CHŌ	跳 N14
CHŌ	丁 E1
CHŌ	朝 F6
CHŌ	町 E1
CHŌ	張 P9
CHŌ	腸 S10
CHŌ	超 O9
CHŌ	鳥 C11
CHŌ	調 L9
CHŌ	挑 N14
CHŌ	澄 T1
CHŌ	彫 L9
CHŌ	聴 F1
CHŌ	潮 F6
CHOKU	勅 J11
CHOKU	直 Z1
CHŪ	駐 I18
CHŪ	宙 D6
CHŪ	鋳 V22
CHŪ	抽 D6
CHŪ	昼 U3
CHŪ	忠 B12
CHŪ	注 I18
CHŪ	仲 B12
CHŪ	虫 B13
CHŪ	柱 I18
CHŪ	中 B12
CHŪ	沖 B12
CHŪ	衷 P5
DA	妥 A11
DA	打 E1
DA	惰 V5
DA	蛇 N9
DA	駄 V9
DA	堕 V2
DAI	大 V9
DAI	第 Y12
DAI	代 W3
DAI	台 Q2
DAI	題 O10
DAKU	諾 V1
DAKU	濁 S3
da(ku)	抱 Y10
dama(ru)	黙 V11
DAN	団 E10
DAN	弾 D13
DAN	断 Z1
DAN	段 Z2
DAN	男 D1
DAN	談 A7
DAN	壇 M1
DAN	暖 V6
dare	誰 G14
da(su)	出 A4
DATSU	脱 B8
DATSU	奪 E10
DEI	泥 U1
DEN	田 D1
DEN	電 N19
DEN	伝 Q5
DEN	殿 U1
de(ru)	出 A4
DO	怒 R8
DO	奴 R8
DO	努 R8
DO	土 I3
DO	度 R1
DŌ	堂 L3
DŌ	同 L8
DŌ	導 E10
DŌ	銅 L8
DŌ	胴 L8
DŌ	動 G3
DŌ	童 M11
DŌ	働 G3
DŌ	洞 L8
DŌ	道 C17
DOKU	独 B13
DOKU	毒 I13
DOKU	読 L4
DON	鈍 N18

DON 曇 Q5
dono 殿 U1
doro 泥 U1
E 会 T2
E 恵 D7
E 絵 T2
e 江 I8
eda 枝 R10
ega(ku) 描 D2
EI 永 P2
EI 英 V18
EI 栄 L2
EI 影 M3
EI 映 V18
EI 鋭 B8
EI 営 L2
EI 泳 P2
EI 詠 P2
EI 衛 G12
EKI 易 S8
EKI 液 S23
EKI 疫 R6
EKI 益 T18
EKI 役 R6
EKI 駅 U3
e(mu) 笑 V13
EN 延 O3
EN 宴 C1
EN 猿 P4
EN 円 L18
EN 園 P4
EN 鉛 T16
EN 援 V6
EN 塩 B1
EN 遠 P4
EN 縁 X5
EN 演 D6
EN 沿 T16
EN 煙 I12
EN 炎 A7
era(bu) 選 Y9
era(i) 偉 F13
eri 襟 J4
e(ru) 獲 R4
e(ru) 得 G11
ETSU 謁 S7
ETSU 悦 B8
ETSU 閲 C8
ETSU 越 W9
FU 不 Z4
FU 譜 I10
FU 附 E11
FU 膚 N16
FU 府 E11
FU 父 A17
FU 夫 V15
FU 賦 W2
FU 符 E11
FU 婦 X4
FU 富 D3
FU 怖 V3
FU 普 I10
FU 浮 A15
FU 負 C19
FU 敷 M6
FU 赴 O9
FU 扶 V15
FU 腐 L7
FU 布 V3
FU 付 E11
FŪ 風 L23
FŪ 夫 V15
FŪ 封 I5
fuchi 縁 X5
fuda 札 N1
fude 筆 X8
fue 笛 D6
fu(eru/yasu) 殖 Z1
fu(eru/yasu) 増 D5
fuka(i) 深 N5
fu(keru/kasu) 更 V8
fu(keru) 老 N9
FUKU 複 S24
FUKU 副 D3
FUKU 腹 S24
FUKU 福 D3
FUKU 幅 D3
FUKU 復 S24
FUKU 服 R1
FUKU 覆 S24
FUKU 伏 V11
fu(ku) 吹 S15
fu(ku) 噴 K1
fuku(mu/meru) 含 T9
fuku(ramu) 膨 I2
fukuro 袋 W3
fu(maeru) 踏 P1
fumi 文 M7
fu(mu) 踏 P1
FUN 憤 K1
FUN 奮 V9
FUN 粉 T14
FUN 噴 K1
FUN 分 T14
FUN 雰 T14
FUN 墳 K1
FUN 紛 T14
fune 舟 L22
fune 船 T16
fu(reru) 触 L18
fu(ru) 降 S23
fu(ru) 振 P10
furu(eru) 震 P10
furu(i) 古 F3
furu(u) 奮 V9
fusa 房 U4
fuse(gu) 防 M6

fushi	節 C9
fu(su/seru)	伏 V11
futa	二 A2
futa	双 R1
futata(bi)	再 L20
futa(tsu)	二 A2
futo(i)	太 V9
futo(ru)	太 V9
FUTSU	払 Q1
FUTSU	沸 Y13
fuyu	冬 S23
GA	芽 E6
GA	我 W7
GA	餓 W7
GA	合 T10
GA	雅 E6
GA	賀 C19
GA	画 D6
GAI	涯 I5
GAI	劾 Q12
GAI	街 I5
GAI	該 Q12
GAI	害 I13
GAI	外 S17
GAI	慨 N8
GAI	概 N8
GAKU	楽 C5
GAKU	額 S26
GAKU	学 L2
GAKU	岳 A21
GAN	岸 F7
GAN	岩 A5
GAN	頑 N6
GAN	願 C6
GAN	丸 N22
GAN	元 N6
GAN	眼 C13
GAN	顔 M20
GAN	含 T9
gara	柄 L7
GATSU	月 L14
GE	外 S17
GE	下 A1
GEI	迎 P16
GEI	芸 Q5
GEI	鯨 M3
GEKI	劇 S11
GEKI	激 M6
GEKI	撃 R6
GEN	元 N6
GEN	幻 Z10
GEN	限 C9
GEN	減 W10
GEN	厳 Z15
GEN	玄 Q15
GEN	言 B2
GEN	現 C18
GEN	弦 Q15
GEN	源 C6
GEN	原 C6
GETSU	月 L14
GI	技 R10
GI	義 W8
GI	議 W8
GI	宜 C15
GI	儀 W8
GI	犠 W8
GI	偽 Z12
GI	欺 S15
GI	戯 W4
GI	擬 O7
GI	疑 O7
GIN	銀 C9
GIN	吟 T9
GO	呉 Y17
GO	護 R4
GO	娯 Y17
GO	碁 K8
GO	後 S23
GO	午 H8
GO	語 I9
GO	御 O4
GO	悟 I9
GO	誤 Y17
GO	互 Z23
GO	五 I9
GŌ	拷 Y15
GŌ	合 T10
GŌ	豪 S11
GŌ	業 J7
GŌ	号 Y14
GŌ	剛 L11
GŌ	強 Q1
GŌ	郷 Q13
GOKU	獄 V11
GON	言 B2
GON	権 H9
GU	愚 L13
GU	具 T18
GŪ	宮 B11
GŪ	遇 L13
GŪ	隅 L13
GŪ	偶 L13
GUN	群 X10
GUN	郡 X10
GUN	軍 L5
GYAKU	逆 Z14
GYAKU	虐 Y1
GYO	形 K2
GYO	魚 D4
GYO	御 O4
GYO	漁 D4
GYŌ	行 G12
GYŌ	暁 K1
GYŌ	仰 P16
GYŌ	業 J7
GYŌ	凝 O7

GYOKU 玉 I17
GYŪ 牛 H1
HA 派 Z7
HA 波 R11
HA 把 N24
HA 法 Q7
HA 破 R11
HA 覇 K5
ha 羽 A22
ha 刃 A10
ha 歯 O1
ha 葉 Z21
haba 幅 D3
haba(mu) 阻 C15
habu(ku) 省 C13
HACHI 鉢 J6
HACHI 八 T14
hada 肌 L23
hadaka 裸 D14
hagane 鋼 L11
hage(mu/masu) 励 S9
hage(shii) 激 M6
haha 母 A16
HAI 肺 M4
HAI 俳 Z3
HAI 背 N12
HAI 廃 T1
HAI 配 Y9
HAI 杯 Z4
HAI 輩 Z3
HAI 排 Z3
HAI 敗 C19
HAI 拝 F10
hai 灰 A7
hai(ru) 入 Z13
haji 恥 A6
haji(maru/meru) 始 Q2
haji(me) 初 A10
haji(ru) 恥 A6
haka 墓 V10
haka(rau) 計 F1
haka(ru) 謀 K7
haka(ru) 量 D12
haka(ru) 計 F1
haka(ru) 測 C20
haka(ru) 図 A18
haka(ru) 諮 S16
hako 箱 C14
hako(bu) 運 L5
HAKU 舶 L22
HAKU 薄 E13
HAKU 拍 C5
HAKU 迫 C5
HAKU 白 C5
HAKU 泊 C5
HAKU 伯 C5
HAKU 博 E13
ha(ku) 掃 X4
ha(ku) 履 U1
ha(ku) 吐 I3
hama 浜 A21
HAN 藩 G5
HAN 班 Z18
HAN 頒 T14
HAN 搬 R6
HAN 煩 A7
HAN 般 R6
HAN 板 R9
HAN 繁 Q16
HAN 販 R9
HAN 畔 F11
HAN 反 R9
HAN 範 N23
HAN 版 Z6
HAN 飯 R9
HAN 帆 L24
HAN 坂 R9
HAN 犯 N23
HAN 半 F11
HAN 判 F11
HAN 伴 F11
HAN 凡 L24
hana 鼻 K3
hana 花 N10
hana 華 Z21
hanaha(dashii) 甚 Y3
hana(reru/su) 離 Q1
hana(su) 話 G2
hana(su) 放 M6
hana(tsu) 放 M6
hane 羽 A22
ha(neru) 跳 N14
hara 原 C6
hara 腹 S24
hara(u) 払 Q1
ha(reru/rasu) 晴 I15
hari 針 F1
haru 春 V21
ha(ru) 張 P9
hasa(maru/mu) 挟 V19
hashi 橋 V13
hashi 端 M11
hashira 柱 I18
hashi(ru) 走 O9
hata 畑 D1
hata 端 M11
hata 旗 M6
hatake 畑 D1
hatara(ku) 働 G3
ha(teru/tasu) 果 D14
HATSU 発 T1
hatsu 初 A10
HATSU 髪 V6
haya(i) 早 F5
haya(i) 速 J11
hayashi 林 J4
ha(zukashii) 恥 A6

hazukashi(meru) 辱 P10
hazu(mu) 弾 D13
hazu(reru/su) 外 S17
hebi 蛇 N9
heda(taru/teru) 隔 Z20
HEI 閉 E9
HEI 幣 Z19
HEI 病 L7
HEI 兵 A21
HEI 並 I10
HEI 陛 N11
HEI 塀 U1
HEI 併 K2
HEI 柄 L7
HEI 丙 L7
HEI 弊 Z19
HEI 平 F9
HEKI 壁 U2
HEKI 癖 U2
HEN 遍 U5
HEN 片 Z6
HEN 返 R9
HEN 辺 A10
HEN 偏 U5
HEN 変 S23
HEN 編 U5
he(ru/rasu) 減 W10
he(ru) 経 R7
HI 卑 F2
HI 避 U2
HI 非 Z3
HI 碑 F2
HI 皮 R11
HI 肥 N24
HI 彼 R11
HI 否 Z4
HI 被 R11
HI 批 N11
HI 披 R11
HI 飛 N2
HI 悲 Z3
HI 疲 R11
HI 泌 N4
HI 扉 Z3
HI 比 N11
HI 罷 Q3
HI 秘 N4
HI 費 Y13
HI 妃 Y9
hi 日 C1
hi 氷 P1
hi 灯 E1
hi 火 A7
hibi(ku) 響 Q13
hidari 左 V5
hi(eru/yasu) 冷 T8
higashi 東 J12
hii(deru) 秀 Z8
hika(eru) 控 N5
hikari 光 A1
hika(ru) 光 A1
hi(keru/ku) 引 Y11
hiki 匹 Y3
hiki(iru) 率 Q15
hi(ku) 弾 D13
hiku(i) 低 P12
hima 暇 Z2
hime 姫 Y5
hi(meru) 秘 N4
HIN 頻 O2
HIN 浜 A21
HIN 貧 T14
HIN 品 B1
HIN 賓 C19
hira 平 F9
hira(ku) 開 K2
hiro(garu/geru) 広 Q4
hiro(i) 広 Q4
hiro(u) 拾 T10
hiru 昼 U3
hirugae(ru/su) 翻 G5
hisa(shii) 久 S22
hiso(mu) 潜 V15
hitai 額 S26
hita(ru/su) 浸 X3
hito 人 A3
hito(ri) 独 B13
hito(shii) 等 E12
hito(tsu) 一 A1
HITSU 泌 N4
HITSU 匹 Y3
HITSU 必 N4
HITSU 筆 X8
hitsuji 羊 F10
HO 舗 T6
HO 浦 L17
HO 歩 O2
HO 捕 L17
HO 補 L17
HO 保 J1
ho 穂 D7
ho 帆 L24
HŌ 豊 D8
HŌ 宝 I17
HŌ 縫 S23
HŌ 褒 P5
HŌ 奉 V21
HŌ 芳 M6
HŌ 胞 Y10
HŌ 砲 Y10
HŌ 崩 L14
HŌ 封 I5
HŌ 泡 Y10
HŌ 飽 Y10
HŌ 峰 S23
HŌ 倣 M6
HŌ 放 M6

HŌ	訪 M6
HŌ	報 R1
HŌ	方 M6
HŌ	抱 Y10
HŌ	法 Q7
HŌ	包 Y10
HŌ	邦 V22
HŌ	俸 V21
hōmu(ru)	葬 S20
hodo	程 I17
hodoko(su)	施 N25
hoga(raka)	朗 C10
hoko	矛 E3
hoko(ru)	誇 Y14
HOKU	北 N12
homa(re)	誉 T18
ho(meru)	褒 P5
HON	奔 K1
HON	翻 G5
HON	本 J6
hone	骨 L10
hone	骨 L10
honō	炎 A7
hora	洞 L8
hori	堀 U1
horo(biru/bosu)	滅 W10
ho(ru)	掘 U1
ho(ru)	彫 L9
hoshi	星 H4
hoso(i)	細 D1
hos(suru)	欲 T17
ho(su)	干 F7
hotaru	蛍 L2
hotoke	仏 Q1
HOTSU	発 T1
HYAKU	百 C7
HYŌ	票 I12
HYŌ	評 F9
HYŌ	表 P5
HYŌ	兵 A21
HYŌ	拍 C5
HYŌ	漂 I12
HYŌ	俵 P5
HYŌ	標 I12
HYŌ	氷 P1
I	位 M11
I	意 M15
I	維 Q16
I	以 P14
I	依 P7
I	尉 U1
I	為 Z12
I	医 Y1
I	胃 D1
I	威 W10
I	緯 F13
I	偉 F13
I	違 F13
I	衣 P7
I	遺 C19
I	移 S17
I	委 G4
I	慰 U1
I	異 K12
I	囲 K9
I	易 S8
i	井 K9
ICHI	一 A1
ICHI	壱 N9
ichi	市 M4
ichijiru(shii)	著 I7
ido(mu)	挑 N14
ie	家 S12
ika(ru)	怒 R8
ike	池 N25
IKI	域 W4
iki	息 C16
ikidō(ru)	憤 K1
ikio(i)	勢 N22
i(kiru/kasu)	生 H4
iko(u)	憩 G2
IKU	育 Q9
iku	幾 W4
ikusa	戦 W4
ima	今 T9
imashi(meru)	戒 W4
i(mawashii)	忌 Y9
imo	芋 E8
imōto	妹 J7
i(mu)	忌 Y9
IN	隠 X1
IN	陰 T9
IN	員 C19
IN	印 Z2
IN	院 N6
IN	姻 V9
IN	韻 M13
IN	飲 S15
IN	引 Y11
IN	因 V9
ina	否 Z4
ine	稲 C4
inochi	命 T8
ino(ru)	祈 A20
inu	犬 V11
iro	色 N24
irodo(ru)	彩 J2
i(reru)	入 Z13
i(ru)	居 U1
i(ru)	鋳 V22
i(ru)	射 Z16
i(ru)	要 I12
isagiyo(i)	潔 Q16
isa(mu)	勇 D1
ishi	石 A5
ishizue	礎 O7

isoga(shii)	忙 M5
iso(gu)	急 X1
ita	板 R9
itadaki	頂 E1
itada(ku)	頂 E1
ita(i)	痛 L16
ita(mu/meru)	傷 S10
ita(mu/meru)	痛 L16
ita(mu)	悼 F5
ita(ru)	至 Q6
ita(su)	致 Q6
ito	糸 Q16
itona(mu)	営 L2
ITSU	逸 S2
ITSU	一 A1
itsuku(shimu)	慈 Q14
itsu(tsu)	五 I9
itsuwa(ru)	偽 Z12
i(u)	言 B2
iwa	岩 A5
iwa(u)	祝 B7
iya(shii)	卑 F2
iya(shimu)	卑 F2
izumi	泉 P1
JA	邪 E6
JA	蛇 N9
JAKU	弱 Y11
JAKU	寂 R3
JAKU	若 V1
JI	字 A15
JI	持 E12
JI	地 N25
JI	寺 E12
JI	次 S16
JI	自 C16
JI	似 P14
JI	児 C4
JI	耳 A6
JI	璽 Z23
JI	磁 Q14
JI	十 F1
JI	侍 E12
JI	滋 Q14
JI	治 Q2
JI	慈 Q14
JI	時 E12
JI	事 X9
JI	示 E7
JI	辞 M17
ji	路 S26
JIKI	直 Z1
JIKU	軸 D6
JIN	陣 C12
JIN	迅 N2
JIN	尋 X1
JIN	神 D11
JIN	甚 Y3
JIN	臣 Y5
JIN	刃 A10
JIN	人 A3
JIN	尽 U3
JIN	仁 A2
JITSU	実 V21
JITSU	日 C1
JO	如 B1
JO	徐 T4
JO	除 T4
JO	女 A11
JO	助 C15
JO	叙 T4
JO	序 E2
JŌ	剰 G9
JŌ	条 S23
JŌ	壌 P6
JŌ	浄 X11
JŌ	乗 G9
JŌ	嬢 P6
JŌ	冗 L23
JŌ	状 V11
JŌ	錠 O6
JŌ	醸 P6
JŌ	場 S10
JŌ	上 A1
JŌ	譲 P6
JŌ	丈 V5
JŌ	城 W11
JŌ	情 I15
JŌ	縄 N19
JŌ	蒸 P1
JŌ	常 L3
JŌ	定 O6
JŌ	畳 L1
JOKU	辱 P10
JU	需 L12
JU	寿 V22
JU	受 R1
JU	授 R1
JU	儒 L12
JU	樹 I2
JŪ	拾 T10
JŪ	獣 V11
JŪ	住 I18
JŪ	重 G3
JŪ	縦 O6
JŪ	渋 O1
JŪ	充 Q10
JŪ	従 O6
JŪ	十 F1
JŪ	汁 F1
JŪ	銃 Q10
JŪ	柔 E3
JUKU	塾 N22
JUKU	熟 N22
JUN	遵 N7
JUN	順 A8
JUN	殉 S20
JUN	准 G14

JUN	循 Z7
JUN	潤 C8
JUN	盾 Z7
JUN	巡 A8
JUN	純 N18
JUN	旬 S6
JUN	準 G14
JUTSU	術 J9
JUTSU	述 J9
KA	河 E4
KA	下 A1
KA	加 B4
KA	果 D14
KA	渦 L10
KA	荷 E4
KA	花 N10
KA	価 I12
KA	夏 S23
KA	架 B4
KA	火 A7
KA	化 N10
KA	暇 Z2
KA	可 E4
KA	靴 N10
KA	佳 I5
KA	菓 D14
KA	課 D14
KA	嫁 S12
KA	過 L10
KA	家 S12
KA	稼 S12
KA	歌 S15
KA	仮 R9
KA	何 E4
KA	寡 Z22
KA	禍 L10
KA	貨 N10
KA	科 F2
KA	箇 F4
KA	華 Z21
ka	日 C1
ka	香 G4
ka	蚊 M7
kabe	壁 U2
kabu	株 H5
kado	角 L18
kado	門 C8
kaeri(miru)	省 C13
kaeri(miru)	顧 U4
kae(ru/su)	帰 Z18
kae(ru/su)	返 R9
kagami	鏡 M13
kagaya(ku)	輝 L5
kage	影 M3
kage(ru)	陰 T9
kagi(ru)	限 C9
KAI	怪 R7
KAI	快 V17
KAI	灰 A7
KAI	海 A16
KAI	悔 A16
KAI	階 N11
KAI	戒 W4
KAI	皆 N11
KAI	改 Y9
KAI	懐 P7
KAI	会 T2
KAI	開 K2
KAI	械 W4
KAI	拐 B1
KAI	絵 T2
KAI	塊 Q11
KAI	界 T3
KAI	解 L18
KAI	海 A16
KAI	回 B1
KAI	壊 P7
KAI	介 T3
kai	貝 C19
kaka(eru)	抱 Y10
kaka(geru)	掲 S7
kakari	係 Q17
ka(karu/keru)	掛 I5
ka(karu/keru)	架 B4
ka(karu/keru)	懸 Z1
kaka(ru)	係 Q17
ka(keru/ku)	欠 S15
ka(keru)	駆 Y2
kaki	垣 C3
kako(mu)	囲 K9
KAKU	隔 Z20
KAKU	革 K5
KAKU	客 S26
KAKU	殻 R6
KAKU	画 D6
KAKU	角 L18
KAKU	郭 M2
KAKU	獲 R4
KAKU	核 Q12
KAKU	各 S26
KAKU	閣 S26
KAKU	較 M9
KAKU	殻 R6
KAKU	拡 Q4
KAKU	覚 L2
KAKU	嚇 I4
KAKU	格 S26
KAKU	確 G14
ka(ku)	書 X8
kaku(reru/su)	隠 X1
kama	窯 N5
kama(eru)	構 L21
kamba(shii)	芳 M6
kami	神 D11
kami	髪 V6
kami	紙 P11
kaminari	雷 D1

KAN	歓 S15
KAN	閑 J1
KAN	鑑 Y6
KAN	管 B10
KAN	喚 S1
KAN	甲 D10
KAN	寛 K3
KAN	観 H9
KAN	刊 F7
KAN	棺 B10
KAN	簡 C8
KAN	缶 H8
KAN	館 B10
KAN	漢 V16
KAN	感 W10
KAN	冠 N6
KAN	寒 T18
KAN	慣 C19
KAN	監 Y6
KAN	憾 W10
KAN	患 B15
KAN	間 C8
KAN	甘 K6
KAN	陥 C4
KAN	汗 F7
KAN	完 N6
KAN	肝 F7
KAN	干 F7
KAN	巻 Y9
KAN	勘 Y3
KAN	款 S15
KAN	還 P4
KAN	艦 Y6
KAN	敢 Z15
KAN	看 G8
KAN	緩 V6
KAN	堪 Y3
KAN	貫 C19
KAN	官 B10
KAN	乾 N2
KAN	幹 T2
KAN	勧 H9
KAN	換 S1
KAN	関 V14
KAN	環 P4
kana(deru)	奏 V21
kanara(zu)	必 N4
kana(shii)	悲 Z3
kana(shimu)	悲 Z3
kane	金 T5
kane	鐘 M11
ka(neru)	兼 X9
kanga(eru)	考 Y15
kanmuri	冠 N6
kao	顔 M20
kao(ri)	香 G4
kao(ru)	薫 G3
kao(ru)	香 G4
kara	空 N5
kara	唐 X6
kara	殻 R6
karada	体 J6
kara(i)	辛 M17
kara(maru/mu)	絡 S26
kare	彼 R11
ka(reru/rasu)	枯 F3
kari	仮 R9
ka(ri)	狩 E10
ka(riru)	借 K11
ka(ru)	刈 A18
ka(ru)	狩 E10
karu(i)	軽 R7
kasa	傘 T2
kasa(naru/neru)	重 G3
kase(gu)	稼 S12
kashiko(i)	賢 Y7
kashira	頭 B6
ka(stu)	且 C15
ka(su)	貸 W3
kata	肩 U4
kata	形 K2
kata	型 K2
kata	潟 Z2
kata	方 M6
kata	片 Z6
katachi	形 K2
kata(i)	堅 Y7
kata(i)	難 V16
kata(i)	硬 V8
kataki	敵 M19
katamari	塊 Q11
katamu(ku/keru)	傾 N10
katana	刀 A10
kata(ru)	語 I9
katawa(ra)	傍 M18
katayo(ru)	偏 U5
kate	糧 D12
KATSU	括 G2
KATSU	滑 L10
KATSU	活 G2
KATSU	喝 S7
KATSU	褐 S7
KATSU	渇 S7
KATSU	割 I13
KATSU	轄 I13
ka(tsu)	勝 V20
katsu(gu)	担 C2
ka(u/wasu)	交 M9
ka(u)	買 C19
ka(u)	飼 Z10
kawa	皮 R11
kawa	側 C20
kawa	川 A8
kawa	河 E4
kawa	革 K5
kawa(ku/kasu)	乾 N2
kawa(ku)	渇 S7

ka(waru/eru) 代 W3
ka(waru/eru) 替 V15
ka(waru/eru) 換 S1
ka(waru/eru) 変 S23
kayo(u) 通 L16
kaza(ru) 飾 T7
kaze 風 L23
kazo(eru) 数 J10
kazu 数 J10
KE 家 S12
KE 気 N2
KE 化 N10
ke 毛 N17
KEI 警 S5
KEI 慶 Z17
KEI 景 M3
KEI 形 K2
KEI 径 R7
KEI 啓 U4
KEI 渓 V15
KEI 軽 R7
KEI 経 R7
KEI 携 Z8
KEI 鶏 V15
KEI 京 M3
KEI 系 Q17
KEI 掲 S7
KEI 型 K2
KEI 継 Z1
KEI 刑 K2
KEI 競 M12
KEI 茎 R7
KEI 係 Q17
KEI 蛍 L2
KEI 敬 S5
KEI 契 I13
KEI 兄 B7
KEI 憩 G2
KEI 計 F1
KEI 恵 D7
KEI 傾 N10
kemono 獣 V11
kemu(ri) 煙 I12
KEN 剣 T11
KEN 謙 X9
KEN 見 C18
KEN 遣 B14
KEN 研 K2
KEN 県 Z1
KEN 肩 U4
KEN 献 V11
KEN 検 T11
KEN 軒 F7
KEN 繭 Z23
KEN 懸 Z1
KEN 建 X8
KEN 険 T11
KEN 絹 B1
KEN 間 C8
KEN 賢 Y7
KEN 兼 X9
KEN 堅 Y7
KEN 犬 V11
KEN 嫌 X9
KEN 件 H1
KEN 健 X8
KEN 倹 T11
KEN 顕 I10
KEN 憲 I13
KEN 験 T11
KEN 権 H9
KEN 券 V20
KEN 圏 Y9
ke(su) 消 L15
KETSU 潔 Q16
KETSU 傑 S18
KETSU 結 I2
KETSU 欠 S15
KETSU 穴 T14
KETSU 決 V17
KETSU 血 A14
kewa(shii) 険 T11
kezu(ru) 削 L15
KI 機 W4
KI 旗 M6
KI 紀 Y9
KI 奇 E5
KI 寄 E5
KI 軌 N20
KI 器 B1
KI 希 V3
KI 祈 A20
KI 輝 L5
KI 汽 N2
KI 既 N8
KI 幾 W4
KI 基 K8
KI 企 T2
KI 帰 Z18
KI 起 Y9
KI 忌 Y9
KI 机 L23
KI 飢 L23
KI 貴 C19
KI 期 K8
KI 記 Y9
KI 騎 E5
KI 己 Y9
KI 棋 K8
KI 規 V15
KI 危 N23
KI 気 N2
KI 季 G4
KI 岐 R10
KI 鬼 Q11
KI 揮 L5
KI 棄 Q8

KI	喜 I2
ki	木 J1
ki	黄 K10
kibi(shii)	厳 Z15
KICHI	吉 I2
ki(eru)	消 L15
KIKU	菊 S3
ki(ku)	聴 F1
ki(ku)	利 G4
ki(ku)	聞 C8
ki(ku)	効 M9
ki(maru/meru)	決 V17
kimi	君 X10
kimo	肝 F7
KIN	禁 J4
KIN	今 T9
KIN	均 S4
KIN	勤 I14
KIN	琴 T9
KIN	緊 Y7
KIN	金 T5
KIN	近 A20
KIN	菌 G4
KIN	謹 I14
KIN	斤 A20
KIN	筋 A9
KIN	襟 J4
kinu	絹 B1
kira(u)	嫌 X9
ki(reru/ru)	切 N15
kiri	霧 E3
ki(ru/seru)	着 I19
kishi	岸 F7
kiso(u)	競 M12
kita	北 N12
kita(eru)	鍛 Z2
kitana(i)	汚 Y14
kita(ru)	来 J10
KITSU	喫 I13
KITSU	吉 I2
KITSU	詰 I2
kiwa	際 R5
kiwa(maru/meru)	極 Y14
kiwa(maru/meru)	窮 Z16
kiwa(meru)	究 N20
kiyo(i)	清 I15
kiza(mu)	刻 Q12
kiza(su)	兆 N14
kizu	傷 S10
kizu(ku)	築 L24
KO	誇 Y14
KO	庫 C12
KO	顧 U4
KO	個 F4
KO	拠 S23
KO	枯 F3
KO	去 Q7
KO	雇 U4
KO	古 F3
KO	戸 U4
KO	鼓 R10
KO	湖 F3
KO	故 F3
KO	孤 Z7
KO	己 Y9
KO	弧 Z7
KO	呼 E8
KO	固 F4
ko	粉 T14
ko	子 A15
ko	小 A12
KŌ	郊 M9
KŌ	候 H7
KŌ	孝 I6
KŌ	甲 D10
KŌ	構 L21
KŌ	巧 Y14
KŌ	公 T15
KŌ	硬 V8
KŌ	綱 L11
KŌ	航 M1
KŌ	香 G4
KŌ	拘 S5
KŌ	講 L21
KŌ	恒 C3
KŌ	衡 G12
KŌ	交 M9
KŌ	鉱 Q4
KŌ	功 I8
KŌ	稿 M2
KŌ	侯 H7
KŌ	皇 I17
KŌ	校 M9
KŌ	紅 I8
KŌ	荒 M5
KŌ	項 I8
KŌ	工 I8
KŌ	口 B1
KŌ	酵 I6
KŌ	攻 I8
KŌ	洪 K12
KŌ	行 G12
KŌ	肯 O1
KŌ	慌 M5
KŌ	光 A1
KŌ	鋼 L11
KŌ	孔 N1
KŌ	江 I8
KŌ	好 A15
KŌ	厚 C1
KŌ	更 V8
KŌ	后 Z7
KŌ	購 L21
KŌ	坑 M1
KŌ	抗 M1
KŌ	耕 K9
KŌ	向 L6

KŌ	興 Z2
KŌ	高 M2
KŌ	効 M9
KŌ	考 Y15
KŌ	溝 L21
KŌ	康 X7
KŌ	幸 F7
KŌ	黄 K10
KŌ	控 N5
KŌ	港 Y9
KŌ	貢 I8
KŌ	広 Q4
KŌ	降 S23
KŌ	絞 M9
KŌß	後 S23
kōmu(ru)	被 R11
kō(ru)	凍 J12
kō(ru)	氷 P1
koba(mu)	拒 Y4
koe	声 U3
ko(eru/yasu)	肥 N24
ko(eru)	越 W9
ko(eru)	超 O9
ko(gareru)	焦 G14
ko(geru/gasu)	焦 G14
kogo(eru)	凍 J12
ko(i)	濃 P10
koi(shii)	恋 M10
kokono(tsu)	九 N20
kokoro	心 N3
kokoro(miru)	試 W1
kokoroyo(i)	快 V17
kokoroza(su)	志 I1
KOKU	国 I17
KOKU	告 H2
KOKU	刻 Q12
KOKU	黒 D12
KOKU	穀 R6
KOKU	谷 T17
KOKU	克 F3
KOKU	酷 H2
koma(kai)	細 D1
koma(ru)	困 J1
kome	米 J10
ko(mu/meru)	込 Z13
KON	婚 P11
KON	魂 Q11
KON	恨 C9
KON	困 J1
KON	懇 S14
KON	混 N11
KON	根 C9
KON	今 T9
KON	金 T5
KON	墾 S14
KON	昆 N11
KON	紺 K6
kona	粉 T14
kono(mu)	好 A15
ko(riru/rashimeru)	懲 I17
koro(bu)	転 Q5
koro(garu/gasu)	転 Q5
koromo	衣 P7
koro(su)	殺 R6
ko(ru/rasu)	凝 O7
koshi	腰 I12
ko(su)	越 W9
ko(su)	超 O9
kota(eru)	答 T10
koto	事 X9
koto	琴 T9
koto	殊 S20
koto	言 B2
koto	異 K12
kotobuki	寿 V22
kotowa(ru)	断 Z1
KOTSU	骨 L10
ko(u)	請 I15
ko(u)	恋 M10
kowa(i)	怖 V3
kowa(su/reru)	壊 P7
koyomi	暦 J4
KU	九 N20
KU	句 S5
KU	苦 F3
KU	工 I8
KU	駆 Y2
KU	区 Y2
KU	口 B1
KŪ	空 N5
kuba(ru)	配 Y9
kubi	首 C17
kuchi	口 B1
kuchibiru	唇 P10
ku(chiru)	朽 Y14
kuda	管 B10
kuda(ku/keru)	砕 N21
kuda(saru)	下 A1
ku(yamu)	悔 A16
kujira	鯨 M3
kuki	茎 R7
kumi	組 C15
kumo	雲 Q5
kumo(ru)	曇 Q5
ku(mu)	組 C15
KUN	勲 G3
KUN	君 X10
KUN	薫 G3
KUN	訓 A8
kuni	国 I17
kura	倉 U6
kura	蔵 Y5
kura(beru)	比 N11
kurai	位 M11
kura(i)	暗 M13
ku(rasu)	暮 V10
kurenai	紅 I8

ku(reru)	暮 V10
kuro	黒 D12
ku(ru)	繰 J3
ku(ru)	来 J10
kuruma	車 C12
kuru(shimu/shimeru)	苦 F3
kuru(u)	狂 I17
kusa	草 F5
kusa(i)	臭 C16
kusari	鎖 C19
kusa(ru/rasu)	腐 L7
kuse	癖 U2
kusuri	薬 C5
KUTSU	屈 U1
KUTSU	掘 U1
kutsu	靴 N10
kutsugae(ru/su)	覆 S24
ku(u)	食 T7
kuwa	桑 R1
kuwada(teru)	企 T2
kuwa(shii)	詳 F10
kuwa(waru/eru)	加 B4
kuya(shii)	悔 A16
kuzu(reru/su)	崩 L14
KYAKU	却 Q7
KYAKU	客 S26
KYAKU	脚 Q7
KYO	挙 T18
KYO	拒 Y4
KYO	居 U1
KYO	巨 Y4
KYO	距 Y4
KYO	去 Q7
KYO	虚 N16
KYO	拠 S23
KYO	許 H8
KYŌ	経 R7
KYŌ	供 K12
KYŌ	恐 L24
KYŌ	境 M13
KYŌ	橋 V13
KYŌ	興 Z2
KYŌ	況 B7
KYŌ	驚 Y8
KYŌ	響 Q13
KYŌ	恭 K12
KYŌ	教 I6
KYŌ	競 M12
KYŌ	協 F1
KYŌ	脅 A9
KYŌ	強 Q1
KYŌ	狂 I17
KYŌ	叫 F2
KYŌ	狭 V19
KYŌ	凶 A19
KYŌ	峡 V19
KYŌ	胸 S3
KYŌ	鏡 M13
KYŌ	矯 V13
KYŌ	挟 V19
KYŌ	郷 Q13
KYŌ	京 M3
KYŌ	共 K12
KYŌ	享 M2
KYOKU	曲 D8
KYOKU	局 Z10
KYOKU	極 Y14
KYŪ	究 N20
KYŪ	急 X1
KYŪ	給 T10
KYŪ	休 J1
KYŪ	糾 F2
KYŪ	丘 A21
KYŪ	窮 Z16
KYŪ	久 S22
KYŪ	救 P3
KYŪ	吸 Z9
KYŪ	球 P3
KYŪ	及 Z9
KYŪ	級 Z9
KYŪ	泣 M11
KYŪ	弓 Y11
KYŪ	求 P3
KYŪ	朽 Y14
KYŪ	宮 B11
KYŪ	九 N20
KYŪ	旧 C4
MA	摩 J5
MA	魔 Q11
MA	麻 J5
MA	磨 J5
ma	間 C8
ma	真 T18
maboroshi	幻 Z10
machi	町 E1
machi	街 I5
mado	窓 Q1
mado(u)	惑 W4
mae	前 L14
ma(garu/geru)	曲 D8
magi(reru/rawasu)	紛 T14
mago	孫 Q17
MAI	毎 A16
MAI	枚 J1
MAI	埋 D12
MAI	米 J10
MAI	妹 J7
mai(ru)	参 Q1
ma(jiru/zeru)	交 M9
makana(u)	賄 V2
maka(su)	任 G6
ma(keru/kasu)ü	負 C19
maki	牧 H1
maki	巻 Y9
makoto	誠 W11
MAKU	幕 V10
MAKU	膜 V10

ma(ku) 巻 Y9
mame 豆 B6
mamo(ru) 守 E10
MAN 万 S9
MAN 漫 R1
MAN 慢 R1
MAN 満 L6
mana(bu) 学 L2
mane(ku) 招 B5
manuka(reru) 免 S2
maru 丸 N22
maru(i) 丸 N22
maru(meru) 丸 N22
masa 正 O5
mastu(ri) 祭 R5
masu 升 G13
ma(su) 増 D5
mata 又 R1
matata(ku) 瞬 S18
mato 的 S4
MATSU 末 J8
MATSU 抹 J8
matsu 松 T15
ma(tsu) 待 G11
matsurigoto 政 O5
matsu(ru) 祭 R5
matta(ku) 全 T2
ma(u) 舞 Z5
mawa(ri) 周 L9
mawa(ru/su) 回 B1
mayo(u) 迷 J10
mayu 繭 Z23
ma(zaru/zeru) 混 N11
mazu(shii) 貧 T14
me 芽 E6
me 目 C13
megu(mu) 恵 D7
megu(ru) 巡 A8
MEI 銘 S19
MEI 鳴 C11
MEI 明 L14
MEI 命 T8
MEI 盟 L14
MEI 名 S19
MEI 迷 J10
mekura 盲 M5
MEN 免 S2
MEN 面 Z23
MEN 綿 C5
meshi 飯 R9
mesu 雌 O1
me(su) 召 B5
METSU 滅 W10
mezura(shii) 珍 T2
MI 味 J7
MI 未 J7
MI 魅 Q11
mi 身 Z16
mi 実 V21
mi 三 A2
michi 道 C17
michibi(ku) 導 E10
mi(chiru/tasu) 満 L6
mida(reru/su) 乱 N1
midori 緑 X5
miga(ku) 磨 J5
migi 右 V1
mijika(i) 短 H7
miji(me) 惨 Q1
miki 幹 T2
mikotonori 詔 B5
mimi 耳 A6
MIN 眠 P13
MIN 民 P13
mina 皆 N11
minami 南 L6
minamoto 源 C6
minato 港 Y9
mine 峰 S23
miniku(i) 醜 Q11
mino(ru) 実 V21
mi(ru/seru) 見 C18
mi(ru) 診 T2
misaki 岬 D10
misasagi 陵 S25
mise 店 B3
mito(meru) 認 A10
MITSU 密 N4
mitsu(gu) 貢 I8
mit(tsu) 三 A2
miya 宮 B11
miyako 都 I7
mizo 溝 L21
mizu 水 P1
mizuka(ra) 自 C16
mizuumi 湖 F3
MO 茂 W9
MO 模 V10
mo 藻 J3
mo 喪 P8
MŌ 盲 M5
MŌ 妄 M5
MŌ 耗 N17
MŌ 望 M5
MŌ 毛 N17
MŌ 網 M5
MŌ 猛 A15
mō(keru) 設 R6
mō(su) 申 D11
mochi(iru) 用 L16
modo(ru/su) 戻 U4
mo(eru/yasu) 燃 V11
mogu(ru) 潜 V15
MOKU 目 C13
MOKU 黙 V11
MOKU 木 J1
momo 桃 N14

MON	問 C8
MON	文 M7
MON	紋 M7
MON	門 C8
MON	聞 C8
monme	匁 S3
mono	物 S8
mono	者 I7
moppa(ra)	専 E13
mori	守 E10
mori	森 J1
mo(ru/rasu)	漏 U1
mo(ru)	盛 W11
moto	本 J6
moto	元 N6
moto	基 K8
moto(meru)	求 P3
MOTSU	物 S8
mo(tsu)	持 E12
motto(mo)	最 R2
moyō(su)	催 G14
MU	無 Z5
MU	務 E3
MU	霧 E3
MU	武 W2
MU	夢 S17
MU	矛 E3
mugi	麦 S23
muka(eru)	迎 P16
mukashi	昔 K11
muko	婿 O7
mu(kō)	向 L6
mu(ku/keru)	向 L6
muku(iru)	報 R1
mune	棟 J12
mune	旨 N13
mune	胸 S3
mura	村 E10
murasaki	紫 Q16
mu(reru)	群 X10
mushi	虫 B13
mu(su)	蒸 P1
musu(bu)	結 I2
musume	娘 C10
mut(tsu)	六 M1
muzuka(shii)	難 V16
MYAKU	脈 Z7
MYŌ	明 L14
MYŌ	命 T8
MYŌ	妙 A13
MYŌ	名 S19
na	菜 J2
na	名 S19
nae	苗 D2
naga(i)	長 P9
naga(i)	永 P2
naga(meru)	眺 N14
naga(reru/su)	流 Q8
nage(ku)	嘆 V16
na(geru)	投 R6
nago(mu)	和 B1
nagu(ru)	殴 Y2
nagusa(mu/meru)	慰 U1
NAI	内 L7
na(i)	亡 M5
na(i)	無 Z5
naka	仲 B12
naka	中 B12
naka(ba)	半 F11
na(ku)	泣 M11
nama(keru)	怠 Q2
namari	鉛 T16
nami	並 I10
nami	波 R11
namida	涙 U4
NAN	男 D1
NAN	軟 S15
NAN	南 L6
NAN	難 V16
nana	七 N15
nana(me)	斜 T4
nana(tsu)	七 N15
nani	何 E4
nao(ru/su)	治 Q2
nao(ru/su)	直 Z1
nara(bu/beru)	並 I10
nara(u)	習 C5
nara(u)	倣 M6
na(reru/rasu)	慣 C19
na(ru/rasu)	鳴 C11
na(ru/su)	成 W11
nasa(ke)	情 I15
natsu	夏 S23
natsuka(shii)	懐 P7
nawa	縄 N19
naya(mu/masu)	悩 A19
ne	音 M13
ne	根 C9
ne	値 Z1
neba(ru)	粘 B3
nega(u)	願 C6
NEI	寧 E1
neko	猫 D2
nemu(i)	眠 P13
nemu(ru)	眠 P13
NEN	燃 V11
NEN	然 V11
NEN	念 T9
NEN	粘 B3
NEN	年 F12
nengo(ro)	懇 S14
ne(ru/kasu)	寝 X3
ne(ru)	練 J12
NETSU	熱 N22
NI	二 A2
NI	児 C4
NI	弐 W2

NI 尼 U1
ni 荷 E4
nibu(ru) 鈍 N18
NICHI 日 C1
ni(eru/ru) 煮 I7
niga(i) 苦 F3
ni(geru/gasu) 逃 N14
nigi(ru) 握 U1
nigo(ru/su) 濁 S3
NIKU 肉 L7
niku(i) 憎 D5
niku(mu) 憎 D5
NIN 任 G6
NIN 認 A10
NIN 人 A3
NIN 妊 G6
NIN 忍 A10
nina(u) 担 C2
ni(ru) 似 P14
nise 偽 Z12
nishi 西 I12
nishi 西 N7
niwa 庭 G7
niwatori 鶏 V15
no 野 E2
NŌ 濃 P10
NŌ 悩 A19
NŌ 脳 A19
NŌ 農 P10
NŌ 納 L7
NŌ 能 Q3
no(beru) 述 J9
no(biru/basu) 延 O3
no(biru/basu) 伸 D11
nobo(ru) 昇 G13
nobo(ru) 登 T1
noga(reru/su) 逃 N14
noki 軒 F7
noko(ru/su) 残 W12
no(mu) 飲 S15
no(ru/seru) 乗 G9
no(ru/seru) 載 W5
nozo(ku) 除 T4
nozo(mu) 望 M5
nozo(mu) 臨 Y5
nu(gu/gasu) 脱 B8
nu(keru/ku) 抜 V6
numa 沼 B5
nuno 布 V3
nu(ru) 塗 T4
nushi 主 I18
nusu(mu) 盗 S16
nu(u) 縫 S23
NYO 女 A11
NYO 如 B1
NYŌ 尿 U1
NYŪ 乳 N1
NYŪ 入 Z13
NYŪ 柔 E3
O 汚 Y14
O 悪 I11
o 尾 U1
Ō 王 I17
Ō 黄 K10
Ō 応 N3
Ō 往 I18
Ō 皇 I17
Ō 奥 L6
Ō 押 D10
Ō 凹 Z23
Ō 横 K10
Ō 欧 Y2
Ō 翁 T15
Ō 殴 Y2
Ō 央 V18
Ō 桜 A11
ōgi 扇 U4
ō(i) 多 S17
ō(kii) 大 V9
ō(se) 仰 P16
ō(u) 覆 S24
ōyake 公 T15
o(biru) 帯 L1
obiya(kasu) 脅 A9
obo(eru) 覚 L2
ochii(ru)/otoshii(reru) 陥 C4
o(chiru/tosu) 落 S26
oda(yaka) 穏 X1
odoro(ku/kasu) 驚 Y8
odo(ru) 踊 L16
odo(ru) 躍 X2
odo(su) 脅 A9
oga(mu) 拝 F10
ogina(u) 補 L17
o(iru) 老 N9
oka 丘 A21
oka(su) 侵 X3
oka(su) 冒 C13
oka(su) 犯 N23
oki 沖 B12
o(kiru/kosu) 起 Y9
okona(u) 行 G12
oko(ru/su) 興 Z2
oko(ru) 怒 R8
o(koru) 起 Y9
okota(ru) 怠 Q2
OKU 屋 U1
OKU 憶 M15
OKU 億 M15
oku 奥 L6
o(ku) 置 Z1
oku(reru/rasu) 遅 U1
oku(ru) 贈 D5
oku(ru) 送 V14
omo 主 I18
omo(i) 重 G3
omomuki 趣 R2

omomu(ku) 赴 O9
omote 表 P5
omote 面 Z23
omo(u) 思 D1
ON 温 C1
ON 穏 X1
ON 音 M13
ON 恩 V9
on 御 O4
ona(ji) 同 L8
oni 鬼 Q11
onna 女 A11
onoono 各 S26
onore 己 Y9
o(reru/ru) 折 A20
o(riru/rosu) 降 S23
oro(ka) 愚 L13
oro(su) 卸 O4
o(ru) 織 W6
osa(eru) 抑 P16
osa(maru/meru) 修 Z23
osa(maru/meru) 収 R1
osa(maru/meru) 治 Q2
osa(maru/meru) 納 L7
osana(i) 幼 Q13
oshi(eru) 教 I6
o(shimu) 惜 K11
osore 虞 Y17
oso(reru) 恐 L24
oso(u) 襲 Y15
oso(waru) 教 I6
osu 雄 V5
o(su) 推 G14
o(su) 押 D10
oto 音 M13
otōto 弟 Y12
otoko 男 D1
otoro(eru) 衰 P5
oto(ru) 劣 A13
otozu(reru) 訪 M6
OTSU 乙 N2
otto 夫 V15
o(u) 追 B9
o(waru/eru) 終 S23
oyo(bu) 及 Z9
oyo(gu) 泳 P2
RA 裸 D14
RA 羅 Q16
RAI 頼 J11
RAI 雷 D1
RAI 礼 N1
RAI 来 J10
RAKU 酪 S26
RAKU 絡 S26
RAKU 楽 C5
RAKU 落 S26
RAN 乱 N1
RAN 濫 Y6
RAN 欄 J12
RAN 覧 Y6
RAN 卵 P16
REI 霊 I10
REI 隷 X7
REI 令 T8
REI 冷 T8
REI 励 S9
REI 鈴 T8
REI 齢 T8
REI 零 T8
REI 礼 N1
REI 麗 Z17
REI 例 S21
REKI 暦 J4
REKI 歴 O1
REN 恋 M10
REN 連 C12
REN 廉 X9
REN 練 J12
REN 錬 J12
RETSU 劣 A13
RETSU 裂 S21
RETSU 烈 S21
RETSU 列 S21
RI 履 U1
RI 利 G4
RI 裏 P5
RI 理 D12
RI 里 D12
RI 離 Q1
RI 吏 V7
RI 痢 G4
RIKI 力 A9
RIKU 陸 I3
RIN 輪 T13
RIN 臨 Y5
RIN 鈴 T8
RIN 厘 D12
RIN 倫 T13
RIN 林 J4
RIN 隣 S18
RITSU 律 X8
RITSU 立 M11
RO 露 S26
RO 炉 U4
RO 路 S26
RŌ 朗 C10
RŌ 老 N9
RŌ 廊 C10
RŌ 浪 C10
RŌ 漏 U1
RŌ 郎 C10
RŌ 労 L2
RŌ 楼 J10
ROKU 六 M1
ROKU 録 X5
RON 論 T13
RUI 塁 I3

RUI 涙 U4
RUI 類 J10
RUI 累 Q16
RYAKU 略 S26
RYO 旅 P4
RYO 虜 N16
RYO 慮 N16
RYŌ 量 D12
RYŌ 料 F2
RYŌ 両 L6
RYŌ 良 C10
RYŌ 領 T8
RYŌ 寮 V12
RYŌ 了 E2
RYŌ 霊 I10
RYŌ 糧 D12
RYŌ 漁 D4
RYŌ 猟 L23
RYŌ 涼 M3
RYŌ 陵 S25
RYŌ 療 V12
RYŌ 僚 V12
RYOKU 緑 X5
RYOKU 力 A9
RYŪ 竜 N19
RYŪ 流 Q8
RYŪ 隆 S23
RYŪ 粒 M11
RYŪ 立 M11
RYŪ 硫 Q8
RYŪ 留 P15
RYŪ 柳 P16
SA 作 H10
SA 差 I19
SA 詐 H10
SA 茶 T2
SA 鎖 C19
SA 唆 S25
SA 砂 A13
SA 査 C15
SA 佐 V5
SA 左 V5
saba(ku) 裁 W5
sabi 寂 R3
sabi(shii) 寂 R3
sachi 幸 F7
sada(maru/meru) 定 O6
saegi(ru) 遮 K4
sa(garu/geru) 下 A1
saga(su) 探 N5
saga(su) 捜 R1
SAI 催 G14
SAI 斎 M8
SAI 彩 J2
SAI 載 W5
SAI 災 A8
SAI 済 M8
SAI 宰 M17
SAI 歳 W10
SAI 妻 X6
SAI 砕 N21
SAI 才 E9
SAI 祭 R5
SAI 西 N7
SAI 最 R2
SAI 債 I16
SAI 裁 W5
SAI 細 D1
SAI 際 R5
SAI 再 L20
SAI 栽 W5
SAI 菜 J2
SAI 採 J2
SAI 西 I12
saiwa(i) 幸 F7
saka 坂 R9
saka(eru) 栄 L2
sakai 境 M13
sakana 魚 D4
saka(rau) 逆 Z14
saka(ru) 盛 W11
sakazuki 杯 Z4
sake 酒 N7
sake(bu) 叫 F2
sa(keru) 避 U2
saki 崎 E5
saki 先 H3
SAKU 索 Q16
SAKU 削 L15
SAKU 作 H10
SAKU 策 L1
SAKU 搾 N5
SAKU 昨 H10
SAKU 冊 L19
SAKU 酢 H10
SAKU 錯 K11
sa(ku/keru) 裂 S21
sa(ku) 咲 V14
sa(ku) 割 I13
sakura 桜 A11
sama 様 P3
samata(geru) 妨 M6
sa(meru/masu) 覚 L2
samu(i) 寒 T18
samurai 侍 E12
SAN 散 K10
SAN 参 Q1
SAN 山 A4
SAN 蚕 V13
SAN 酸 S25
SAN 惨 Q1
SAN 賛 V15
SAN 産 M20
SAN 傘 T2
SAN 算 K3
SAN 桟 W12
SAN 三 A2

sara	皿 A14
sara	更 V8
saru	猿 P4
sa(ru)	去 Q7
sasa(eru)	支 R10
sa(saru/su)	刺 L1
saso(u)	誘 Z8
sa(su)	差 I19
sa(su)	指 N13
sa(su)	挿 G3
sato	里 D12
sato(ru)	悟 I9
sato(su)	諭 T12
SATSU	擦 R5
SATSU	札 N1
SATSU	撮 R2
SATSU	冊 L19
SATSU	刷 U1
SATSU	殺 R6
SATSU	察 R5
sawa	沢 U3
sawa(gu)	騒 R1
sawa(ru)	触 L18
sawa(ru)	障 M14
sazu(karu/keru)	授 R1
SE	施 N25
SE	世 Z21
se	畝 S22
se	瀬 J11
se	背 N12
SEI	政 O5
SEI	姓 H4
SEI	性 H4
SEI	勢 N22
SEI	婿 O7
SEI	情 I15
SEI	制 H1
SEI	精 I15
SEI	青 I15
SEI	省 C13
SEI	盛 W11
SEI	生 H4
SEI	正 O5
SEI	征 O5
SEI	請 I15
SEI	聖 I17
SEI	斉 M8
SEI	成 W11
SEI	声 U3
SEI	世 Z21
SEI	誠 W11
SEI	整 O5
SEI	西 N7
SEI	静 X11
SEI	井 K9
SEI	星 H4
SEI	誓 B2
SEI	逝 A20
SEI	牲 H4
SEI	西 I12
SEI	製 P7
SEI	晴 I15
SEI	清 I15
SEKI	斥 A20
SEKI	夕 S17
SEKI	昔 K11
SEKI	席 K4
SEKI	析 A20
SEKI	隻 R4
SEKI	赤 I4
SEKI	籍 K11
SEKI	跡 M10
SEKI	石 A5
SEKI	積 I16
SEKI	責 I16
SEKI	績 I16
SEKI	惜 K11
seki	関 V14
sema(i)	狭 V19
sema(ru)	迫 C5
se(meru)	責 I16
se(meru)	攻 I8
SEN	宣 C3
SEN	仙 A4
SEN	染 N20
SEN	船 T16
SEN	旋 O7
SEN	繊 W5
SEN	践 W12
SEN	潜 V15
SEN	遷 Y9
SEN	戦 W4
SEN	線 P1
SEN	銑 H3
SEN	扇 U4
SEN	泉 P1
SEN	選 Y9
SEN	占 B3
SEN	栓 T2
SEN	銭 W12
SEN	千 G1
SEN	川 A8
SEN	洗 H3
SEN	鮮 F10
SEN	薦 Z17
SEN	専 E13
SEN	先 H3
SEN	浅 W12
se(ru)	競 M12
SETSU	摂 A6
SETSU	節 C9
SETSU	切 N15
SETSU	拙 A4
SETSU	設 R6
SETSU	窃 N15
SETSU	接 M11
SETSU	雪 X1

SETSU 折 A20
SETSU 説 B8
SHA 赦 I4
SHA 謝 Z16
SHA 車 C12
SHA 斜 T4
SHA 写 Y16
SHA 捨 T6
SHA 射 Z16
SHA 舎 T6
SHA 社 I3
SHA 者 I7
SHA 砂 A13
SHA 遮 K4
SHA 煮 I7
SHAKU 尺 U3
SHAKU 借 K11
SHAKU 赤 I4
SHAKU 釈 U3
SHAKU 酌 S4
SHAKU 爵 E10
SHAKU 勺 S4
SHI 詩 E12
SHI 私 Q1
SHI 市 M4
SHI 史 V7
SHI 視 C18
SHI 氏 P11
SHI 祉 O1
SHI 詞 Z10
SHI 嗣 Z10
SHI 資 S16
SHI 諮 S16
SHI 肢 R10
SHI 支 R10
SHI 指 N13
SHI 示 E7
SHI 試 W1
SHI 自 C16
SHI 脂 N13
SHI 誌 I1
SHI 姿 S16
SHI 紫 Q16
SHI 旨 N13
SHI 使 V7
SHI 次 S16
SHI 姉 M4
SHI 賜 S8
SHI 置 Z1
SHI 伺 Z10
SHI 四 B1
SHI 枝 R10
SHI 師 B9
SHI 刺 L1
SHI 子 A15
SHI 糸 Q16
SHI 志 I1
SHI 紙 P11
SHI 矢 H7
SHI 始 Q2
SHI 仕 I1
SHI 司 Z10
SHI 士 I1
SHI 歯 O1
SHI 思 D1
SHI 飼 Z10
SHI 止 O1
SHI 雌 O1
SHI 至 Q6
SHI 施 N25
shiawa(se) 幸 F7
shiba 芝 Z11
shiba(ru) 縛 E13
shibo(ru) 搾 N5
shibo(ru) 絞 M9
shibu(i) 渋 O1
shibu(ru) 渋 O1
SHICHI 七 N15
SHICHI 質 C19
shige(ru) 茂 W9
shiita(geru) 虐 Y1
SHIKI 織 W6
SHIKI 色 N24
SHIKI 式 W1
SHIKI 識 W6
shi(ku) 敷 M6
shima 島 C11
shi(maru/meru) 絞 M9
shi(maru/meru) 閉 E9
shi(maru/meru) 締 M18
shime(ru/su) 湿 I10
shi(meru) 占 B3
shime(su) 示 E7
shi(miru) 染 N20
shimo 霜 C14
SHIN 震 P10
SHIN 診 T2
SHIN 浸 X3
SHIN 身 Z16
SHIN 真 T18
SHIN 娠 P10
SHIN 慎 T18
SHIN 申 D11
SHIN 進 G14
SHIN 深 N5
SHIN 新 M16
SHIN 親 M16
SHIN 信 B2
SHIN 唇 P10
SHIN 津 X8
SHIN 辛 M17
SHIN 薪 M16
SHIN 心 N3
SHIN 針 F1
SHIN 森 J1
SHIN 神 D11
SHIN 臣 Y5

SHIN	紳 D11
SHIN	寝 X3
SHIN	伸 D11
SHIN	審 G5
SHIN	振 P10
SHIN	侵 X3
shina	品 B1
shino(bu)	忍 A10
shi(nu)	死 S20
shio	潮 F6
shio	塩 B1
shira(beru)	調 L9
shirizo(ku/keru)	退 C9
shiro	白 C5
shiro	城 W11
shiro(i)	白 C5
shiru	汁 F1
shi(ru)	知 H7
shirushi	印 Z2
shiru(su)	記 Y9
shita	舌 G2
shita	下 A1
shitaga(u/eru)	従 O6
shita(shii)	親 M16
shita(shimu)	親 M16
shitata(ru)	滴 M19
shita(u)	慕 V10
SHITSU	湿 I10
SHITSU	質 C19
SHITSU	疾 H7
SHITSU	漆 T2
SHITSU	室 Q6
SHITSU	失 H6
SHITSU	執 N22
shizu(ka)	静 X11
shizuku	滴 M19
shizu(maru/meru)	鎮 T18
shizu(maru/meru)	静 X11
shizu(mu/meru)	沈 N8
SHO	諸 I7
SHO	緒 I7
SHO	庶 K4
SHO	処 S23
SHO	暑 I7
SHO	初 A10
SHO	所 U4
SHO	署 I7
SHO	書 X8
SHŌ	詔 B5
SHŌ	奨 E10
SHŌ	礁 G14
SHŌ	将 E10
SHŌ	尚 L6
SHŌ	掌 L3
SHŌ	晶 C1
SHŌ	象 S11
SHŌ	紹 B5
SHŌ	症 O5
SHŌ	昭 B5
SHŌ	沼 B5
SHŌ	訟 T15
SHŌ	詳 F10
SHŌ	渉 O2
SHŌ	祥 F10
SHŌ	称 A12
SHŌ	硝 L15
SHŌ	笑 V13
SHŌ	衝 G12
SHŌ	肖 L15
SHŌ	焼 K1
SHŌ	匠 Y1
SHŌ	招 B5
SHŌ	抄 A13
SHŌ	召 B5
SHŌ	賞 L3
SHŌ	粧 I3
SHŌ	章 M14
SHŌ	宵 L15
SHŌ	勝 V20
SHŌ	鐘 M11
SHŌ	商 M19
SHŌ	傷 S10
SHŌ	彰 M14
SHŌ	照 B5
SHŌ	松 T15
SHŌ	升 G13
SHŌ	精 I15
SHŌ	償 L3
SHŌ	消 L15
SHŌ	政 O5
SHŌ	唱 C1
SHŌ	性 H4
SHŌ	証 O5
SHŌ	姓 H4
SHŌ	省 C13
SHŌ	生 H4
SHŌ	少 A13
SHŌ	障 M14
SHŌ	昇 G13
SHŌ	小 A12
SHŌ	承 P1
SHŌ	床 J1
SHŌ	星 H4
SHŌ	焦 G14
SHŌ	装 P7
SHŌ	相 C14
SHŌ	正 O5
SHOKU	職 W6
SHOKU	食 T7
SHOKU	植 Z1
SHOKU	嘱 U1
SHOKU	触 L18
SHOKU	飾 T7
SHOKU	織 W6
SHOKU	色 N24
SHOKU	殖 Z1
SHU	酒 N7

SHU 趣 R2
SHU 朱 H5
SHU 守 E10
SHU 主 I18
SHU 狩 E10
SHU 種 G3
SHU 殊 S20
SHU 首 C17
SHU 手 G8
SHU 珠 H5
SHU 取 R2
SHŪ 州 A8
SHŪ 愁 A7
SHŪ 秀 Z8
SHŪ 臭 C16
SHŪ 習 C5
SHŪ 拾 T10
SHŪ 襲 Y15
SHŪ 衆 P4
SHŪ 周 L9
SHŪ 執 N22
SHŪ 秋 A7
SHŪ 集 G14
SHŪ 舟 L22
SHŪ 収 R1
SHŪ 修 Z23
SHŪ 酬 A8
SHŪ 週 L9
SHŪ 宗 E7
SHŪ 就 N8
SHŪ 終 S23
SHŪ 囚 A3
SHŪ 醜 Q11
SHUKU 宿 C7
SHUKU 縮 C7
SHUKU 叔 R3
SHUKU 淑 R3
SHUKU 粛 X7
SHUKU 祝 B7
SHUN 春 V21
SHUN 瞬 S18
SHUN 俊 S25
SHUTSU 出 A4
SO 措 K11
SO 訴 A20
SO 租 C15
SO 疎 O7
SO 礎 O7
SO 阻 C15
SO 組 C15
SO 素 Q16
SO 祖 C15
SO 粗 C15
SO 塑 Z14
SŌ 窓 Q1
SŌ 奏 V21
SŌ 装 P7
SŌ 相 C14
SŌ 争 X11
SŌ 早 F5
SŌ 葬 S20
SŌ 送 V14
SŌ 槽 D9
SŌ 宗 E7
SŌ 双 R1
SŌ 壮 I1
SŌ 想 C14
SŌ 巣 D14
SŌ 喪 P8
SŌ 草 F5
SŌ 掃 X4
SŌ 捜 R1
SŌ 燥 J3
SŌ 層 U1
SŌ 曹 D9
SŌ 僧 D5
SŌ 倉 U6
SŌ 桑 R1
SŌ 騒 R1
SŌ 走 O9
SŌ 創 U6
SŌ 霜 C14
SŌ 遭 D9
SŌ 操 J3
SŌ 挿 G3
SŌ 荘 I1
SŌ 総 T15
SŌ 藻 J3
sōrō 候 H7
soda(tsu/teru) 育 Q9
soko 底 P12
soko(nau/neru) 損 C19
SOKU 束 J11
SOKU 測 C20
SOKU 速 J11
SOKU 息 C16
SOKU 則 C20
SOKU 即 C9
SOKU 促 O8
SOKU 側 C20
SOKU 足 O8
so(maru/meru) 染 N20
somu(ku/keru) 背 N12
SON 尊 N7
SON 存 V4
SON 孫 Q17
SON 村 E10
SON 損 C19
sona(eru) 供 K12
sona(waru/eru) 備 L16
sono 園 P4
sora 空 N5
so(ru/rasu) 反 R9
soso(gu) 注 I18
sosonoka(su) 唆 S25
soto 外 S17
SOTSU 率 Q15

SOTSU 卒 M1
so(u/eru) 添 V13
so(u) 沿 T16
SU 素 Q16
SU 子 A15
su 酢 H10
su 州 A8
su 巣 D14
SŪ 崇 E7
SŪ 数 J10
SŪ 枢 Y2
sube(ru) 滑 L10
sude(ni) 既 N8
sue 末 J8
su(eru) 据 U1
sugata 姿 S16
sugi 杉 J1
su(giru) 過 L10
sugu(reru) 優 Z22
SUI 水 P1
SUI 粋 N21
SUI 錘 G10
SUI 穂 D7
SUI 垂 G10
SUI 推 G14
SUI 帥 B9
SUI 衰 P5
SUI 炊 S15
SUI 酔 N21
SUI 吹 S15
SUI 遂 S13
SUI 睡 G10
suji 筋 A9
suko(shi) 少 A13
suko(yaka) 健 X8
su(ku/kasu) 透 Z8
su(ku) 好 A15
suku(nai) 少 A13
suku(u) 救 P3
sumi 炭 A7
sumi 墨 D12
sumi 隅 L13
sumi(yaka) 速 J11
su(mu/masu) 済 M8
su(mu/masu) 澄 T1
su(mu) 住 I18
SUN 寸 E10
suna 砂 A13
su(ru/reru) 擦 R5
su(ru) 刷 U1
surudo(i) 鋭 B8
susu(meru) 薦 Z17
susu(meru) 勧 H9
susu(mu/meru) 進 G14
suta(ru/reru) 廃 T1
su(teru) 捨 T6
su(u) 吸 Z9
suwa(ru) 座 A3
suzu 鈴 T8
suzu(mu) 涼 M3
suzu(shii) 涼 M3
TA 太 V9
TA 多 S17
TA 他 N25
ta 田 D1
taba 束 J11
ta(beru) 食 T7
tabi 度 R1
tabi 旅 P4
tada(shi) 但 C2
tada(su) 正 O5
tadayo(u) 漂 I12
ta(eru) 耐 L12
ta(eru) 堪 Y3
taga(i) 互 Z23
tagaya(su) 耕 K9
TAI 待 G11
TAI 耐 L12
TAI 代 W3
TAI 帯 L1
TAI 体 J6
TAI 太 V9
TAI 大 V9
TAI 滞 L1
TAI 台 Q2
TAI 退 C9
TAI 逮 X7
TAI 泰 V21
TAI 袋 W3
TAI 態 Q3
TAI 貸 W3
TAI 胎 Q2
TAI 怠 Q2
TAI 替 V15
TAI 対 M7
TAI 隊 S13
tai(ra) 平 F9
taka(i) 高 M2
takara 宝 I17
take 丈 V5
take 岳 A21
take 竹 H11
taki 滝 N19
takigi 薪 M16
TAKU 沢 U3
TAKU 択 U3
TAKU 託 N15
TAKU 濯 X2
TAKU 拓 A5
TAKU 宅 N15
TAKU 卓 F5
ta(ku) 炊 S15
taku(mi) 巧 Y14
takuwa(eru) 蓄 Q15
tama 霊 I10
tama 球 P3
tama 弾 D13

tama 玉 I17
tamago 卵 P16
tamashii 魂 Q11
tamawa(ru) 賜 S8
ta(meru) 矯 V13
tame(su) 試 W1
tami 民 P13
tamo(tsu) 保 J1
TAN 単 D13
TAN 嘆 V16
TAN 担 C2
TAN 淡 A7
TAN 胆 C2
TAN 鍛 Z2
TAN 炭 A7
TAN 短 H7
TAN 端 M11
TAN 丹 L22
TAN 誕 O3
TAN 探 N5
tana 棚 L14
tane 種 G3
tani 谷 T17
tano(mu) 頼 J11
tano(shii) 楽 C5
tao(su/reru) 倒 Q6
ta(reru/rasu) 垂 G10
ta(riru/su) 足 O8
tashi(ka) 確 G14
tashi(kameru) 確 G14
tasu(karu/keru) 助 C15
tataka(u) 闘 E10
tataka(u) 戦 W4
tata(mi) 畳 L1
tate 盾 Z7
tate 縦 O6
tatematsu(ru) 奉 V21
tato(eru) 例 S21
ta(tsu/teru) 建 X8
ta(tsu/teru) 立 M11
ta(tsu/yasu) 絶 N24
TATSU 達 F10
tatsu 竜 N19
ta(tsu) 断 Z1
ta(tsu) 裁 W5
tatto(i) 貴 C19
tatto(i) 尊 N7
tawamu(reru) 戯 W4
tawara 俵 P5
tayo(ri) 便 V8
tayo(ru) 頼 J11
tazu(neru) 尋 X1
tazu(neru) 訪 M6
tazusa(waru) 携 Z8
te 手 G8
TEI 庭 G7
TEI 堤 O10
TEI 低 P12
TEI 程 I17
TEI 呈 I17
TEI 丁 E1
TEI 定 O6
TEI 帝 M18
TEI 貞 C19
TEI 締 M18
TEI 底 P12
TEI 邸 P12
TEI 抵 P12
TEI 弟 Y12
TEI 艇 L22
TEI 廷 G7
TEI 停 M2
TEI 偵 C19
TEI 訂 E1
TEI 逓 Z7
TEI 提 O10
TEI 亭 M2
TEKI 摘 M19
TEKI 適 M19
TEKI 滴 M19
TEKI 的 S4
TEKI 笛 D6
TEKI 敵 M19
TEN 点 B3
TEN 典 D8
TEN 転 Q5
TEN 天 V13
TEN 店 B3
TEN 殿 U1
TEN 添 V13
TEN 展 U1
tera 寺 E12
te(ru/rasu) 照 B5
TETSU 迭 H6
TETSU 鉄 H6
TETSU 徹 Q9
TETSU 撤 Q9
TETSU 哲 B1
TO 図 A18
TO 斗 F2
TO 吐 I3
TO 登 T1
TO 途 T4
TO 徒 O9
TO 塗 T4
TO 土 I3
TO 渡 R1
TO 都 I7
to 戸 U4
TŌ 灯 E1
TŌ 塔 T10
TŌ 頭 B6
TŌ 搭 T10
TŌ 踏 P1
TŌ 凍 J12
TŌ 筒 L8
TŌ 豆 B6

TŌ 東 J12
TŌ 盗 S16
TŌ 桃 N14
TŌ 痘 B6
TŌ 投 R6
TŌ 党 L3
TŌ 陶 S3
TŌ 糖 X6
TŌ 逃 N14
TŌ 島 C11
TŌ 到 Q6
TŌ 冬 S23
TŌ 倒 Q6
TŌ 悼 F5
TŌ 謄 V20
TŌ 湯 S10
TŌ 闘 E10
TŌ 登 T1
TŌ 統 Q10
TŌ 騰 V20
TŌ 刀 A10
TŌ 稲 C4
TŌ 棟 J12
TŌ 当 X1
TŌ 等 E12
TŌ 討 E10
TŌ 唐 X6
TŌ 答 T10
TŌ 透 Z8
tō 十 F1
tōge 峠 A4
tō(i) 遠 P4
tō(ru/su) 通 L16
tōto(bu) 尊 N7
tobira 扉 Z3
tobo(shii) 乏 Z11
to(bu/basu) 飛 N2
to(bu) 跳 N14
todokō(ru) 滞 L1
todo(ku/deru) 届 U1
to(geru) 遂 S13
to(gu) 研 K2
to(jiru/zasu) 閉 E9
to(keru/kasu) 溶 T17
toki 時 E12
toko 床 J1
tokoro 所 U4
TOKU 篤 Y8
TOKU 徳 G11
TOKU 督 R3
TOKU 得 G11
TOKU 匿 Y1
TOKU 特 H1
to(ku) 解 L18
to(ku) 説 B8
to(maru/meru) 泊 C5
to(maru/meru) 止 O1
to(maru/meru) 留 P15
tomi 富 D3
tomo 友 V6
tomo 共 K12
tomo 供 K12
tomona(u) 伴 F11
to(mu) 富 D3
tomura(u) 弔 Y12
TON 豚 S11
TON 屯 N18
tona(eru) 唱 C1
tonari 隣 S18
tono 殿 U1
tori 鳥 C11
to(ru) 採 J2
to(ru) 捕 L17
to(ru) 取 R2
to(ru) 撮 R2
to(ru) 執 N22
toshi 年 F12
totono(u/eru) 整 O5
TOTSU 突 N5
TOTSU 凸 Z23
totsu(gu) 嫁 S12
to(u) 問 C8
TSU 都 I7
TSŪ 痛 L16
TSŪ 通 L16
tsu 津 X8
tsubasa 翼 K12
tsubo 坪 F9
tsubu 粒 M11
tsuchi 土 I3
tsuchika(u) 培 M12
tsudo(u) 集 G14
tsu(geru) 告 H2
tsugi 次 S16
tsu(gu) 接 M11
tsu(gu) 次 S16
tsu(gu) 継 Z1
tsuguna(u) 償 L3
TSUI 対 M7
TSUI 墜 S13
TSUI 追 B9
tsui(yasu) 費 Y13
tsuka 塚 S11
tsuka(eru) 仕 I1
tsuka(maru/maeru) 捕 L17
tsuka(reru) 疲 R11
tsu(karu/keru) 漬 I16
tsuka(u/wasu) 遣 B14
tsuka(u) 使 V7
tsuki 月 L14
tsu(kiru/kusu) 尽 U3
tsu(ku/keru) 着 I19
tsu(ku/keru) 付 E11
tsu(ku/keru) 就 N8
tsu(ku) 突 N5
tsukue 机 L23
tsukuro(u) 繕 I19

Reading	Kanji	Ref.
tsuku(ru)	作	H10
tsuku(ru)	造	H2
tsuma	妻	X6
tsu(maru/meru)	詰	I2
tsume(tai)	冷	T8
tsumi	罪	Z3
tsu(moru/mu)	積	I16
tsumu	錘	G10
tsu(mu)	摘	M19
tsumu(gu)	紡	M6
tsuna	綱	L11
tsune	常	L3
tsuno	角	L18
tsuno(ru)	募	V10
tsura	面	Z23
tsura(naru/neru)	連	C12
tsuranu(ku)	貫	C19
tsu(reru)	連	C12
tsuru	弦	Q15
tsu(ru)	釣	S4
tsurugi	剣	T11
tsuta(waru/eru)	伝	Q5
tsuto(maru/meru)	勤	I14
tsuto(meru)	努	R8
tsuto(meru)	務	E3
tsutsu	筒	L8
tsutsumi	堤	O10
tsutsu(mu)	包	Y10
tsutsushi(mu)	謹	I14
tsutsushi(mu)	慎	T18
tsuyo(i)	強	Q1
tsuyu	露	S26
tsuzu(ku/keru)	続	L4
tsuzumi	鼓	R10
U	羽	A22
U	宇	E8
U	有	V2
U	右	V1
U	雨	L6
uba(u)	奪	E10
uchi	内	L7
ude	腕	S17
ue	上	A1
u(eru)	飢	L23
ugo(ku/kasu)	動	G3
uji	氏	P11
ukaga(u)	伺	Z10
u(kareru)	浮	A15
u(karu)	受	R1
u(keru)	請	I15
u(keru)	受	R1
uketamawa(ru)	承	P1
u(ku)	浮	A15
uma	馬	Y8
u(mareru/mu)	産	M20
u(maru/meru)	埋	D12
ume	梅	A16
umi	海	A16
u(mu)	生	H4
UN	運	L5
UN	雲	Q5
unaga(su)	促	O8
une	畝	S22
ura	浦	L17
ura	裏	P5
ura(meshii)	恨	C9
ura(mu)	恨	C9
urana(u)	占	B3
ure(eru)	憂	Z22
ure(i)	愁	A7
ure(i)	憂	Z22
u(reru)	熟	N22
u(ru)	得	G11
u(ru)	売	L4
uruo(u/su)	潤	C8
urushi	漆	T2
uruwa(shii)	麗	Z17
ushi	牛	H1
ushina(u)	失	H6
ushi(ro)	後	S23
usu(i)	薄	E13
uta	歌	S15
utaga(u)	疑	O7
uta(u)	歌	S15
uta(u)	謡	F8
uto(i)	疎	O7
uto(mu)	疎	O7
u(tsu)	討	E10
u(tsu)	撃	R6
u(tsu)	打	E1
utsuku(shii)	美	I19
utsu(ru/su)	移	S17
utsu(ru/su)	映	V18
utsu(ru/su)	写	Y16
utsuwa	器	B1
utta(eru)	訴	A20
u(waru/eru)	植	Z1
uyama(u)	敬	S5
uyauya(shii)	恭	K12
uzu	渦	L10
WA	和	B1
WA	話	G2
wa	輪	T13
WAI	賄	V2
waka(i)	若	V1
waka(reru)	別	S9
wa(karu)	分	T14
wake	訳	U3
wa(keru)	分	T14
WAKU	惑	W4
waku	枠	N21
wa(ku/kasu)	沸	Y13
WAN	腕	S17
WAN	湾	Y11
warabe	童	M11
wara(u)	笑	V13
ware	我	W7

wa(ru/reru) 割 I13
waru(i) 悪 I11
wasu(reru) 忘 M5
wata 綿 C5
wata(ru/su) 渡 R1
watashi 私 Q1
waza 業 J7
waza 技 R10
wazawa(i) 災 A8
wazura(u/wasu) 煩 A7
wazura(u) 患 B15
YA 野 E2
YA 夜 S23
ya 屋 U1
ya 矢 H7
ya 家 S12
yabu(reru/ru) 破 R11
yabu(reru) 敗 C19
yado 宿 C7
yado(ru/su) 宿 C7
ya(keru/ku) 焼 K1
YAKU 躍 X2
YAKU 約 S4
YAKU 厄 N23
YAKU 役 R6
YAKU 薬 C5
YAKU 訳 U3
yama 山 A4
yamai 病 L7
ya(meru) 辞 M17
ya(mu) 病 L7
yanagi 柳 P16
yasa(shii) 易 S8
yasa(shii) 優 Z22
yashina(u) 養 I19
yashiro 社 I3
yasu(i) 安 A11
yasu(mu/meru) 休 J1
yato(u) 雇 U4
ya(tsu) 八 T14
yat(tsu) 八 T14
yawa(ragu/rageru) 和 B1
yawa(raka) 軟 S15
yawa(raka) 柔 E3
YO 預 E2
YO 余 T4
YO 予 E2
YO 与 Y16
yo 世 Z21
yo 夜 S23
YŌ 庸 X6
YŌ 踊 L16
YŌ 曜 X2
YŌ 陽 S10
YŌ 葉 Z21
YŌ 養 I19
YŌ 容 T17
YŌ 洋 F10
YŌ 揺 F8
YŌ 様 P3
YŌ 用 L16
YŌ 羊 F10
YŌ 幼 Q13
YŌ 腰 I12
YŌ 窯 N5
YŌ 擁 Q13
YŌ 謡 F8
YŌ 揚 S10
YŌ 誉 T18
YŌ 要 I12
YŌ 溶 T17
yo(bu) 呼 E8
yogo(reru/su) 汚 Y14
yoi 宵 L15
yo(i) 良 C10
yo(i) 善 I19
yoko 横 K10
YOKU 浴 T17
YOKU 抑 P16
YOKU 欲 T17
YOKU 翼 K12
YOKU 翌 M11
yome 嫁 S12
yo(mu) 詠 P2
yo(mu) 読 L4
yon 四 B1
yoroko(bu) 喜 I2
yo(ru/seru) 寄 E5
yoru 夜 S23
yo(ru) 因 V9
yoshi 由 D6
yosō(u) 装 P7
yot(tsu) 四 B1
yo(u) 酔 N21
yowa(i) 弱 Y11
yowa(ru) 弱 Y11
YU 癒 T12
YU 油 D6
YU 輸 T12
YU 愉 T12
YU 由 D6
YU 遊 M6
YU 諭 T12
yu 湯 S10
YŪ 有 V2
YŪ 勇 D1
YŪ 裕 T17
YŪ 郵 G10
YŪ 猶 N7
YŪ 幽 Q14
YŪ 由 D6
YŪ 融 Z20
YŪ 雄 V5
YŪ 右 V1
YŪ 友 V6
YŪ 遊 M6
YŪ 悠 N3

YŪ	憂 Z22	ZA	座 A3	ZETSU	舌 G2
YŪ	優 Z22	ZAI	財 E9	ZŌ	憎 D5
YŪ	誘 Z8	ZAI	在 V4	ZŌ	造 H2
yū	夕 S17	ZAI	材 E9	ZŌ	像 S11
yubi	指 N13	ZAI	罪 Z3	ZŌ	象 S11
yue	故 F3	ZAI	剤 M8	ZŌ	蔵 Y5
YUI	遺 C19	ZAN	惨 Q1	ZŌ	臓 Y5
YUI	唯 G14	ZAN	暫 C12	ZŌ	雑 N20
yuka	床 J1	ZAN	残 W12	ZŌ	贈 D5
yuki	雪 X1	ZATSU	雑 N20	ZŌ	増 D5
yu(ku)	行 G12	ZE	是 O10	ZOKU	俗 T17
yu(ku)	逝 A20	ZEI	税 B8	ZOKU	属 U1
yume	夢 S17	ZEN	善 I19	ZOKU	族 M6
yumi	弓 Y11	ZEN	漸 C12	ZOKU	賊 W4
yu(reru)	揺 F8	ZEN	繕 I19	ZOKU	続 L4
yuru(mu/meru)	緩 V6	ZEN	然 V11	ZON	存 V4
yuru(su)	許 H8	ZEN	前 L14	ZU	頭 B6
yuru(yaka)	緩 V6	ZEN	禅 D13	ZU	図 A18
yuta(ka)	豊 D8	ZEN	全 T2	ZUI	髄 V2
yu(u)	結 I2	zeni	銭 W12	ZUI	随 V2
yuzu(ru)	譲 P6	ZETSU	絶 N24		

Historical Radicals (198)
LE1 - LE24, RI1 - RI8, TO2, TO5 - TO8, TO10, TO12, BO2 - BO5, BG1 - BG6, FR1, FR3 - FR7, A1 - A12, A14 - A17, A19, A20, A22, B1, B2, B6, B13, C1, C5, C8, C9, C12, C13, C16 - C19, D1, D4, D12, E3, E6, E7, E10, F1, F2, F7, F10, F13, G2, G4, G5, G8, G11, G12, G14, H1, H4, H7, H11, I1, I3, I4, I8, I12, I15, I17, J1, J5, J10, K3, K5, K6, L1, L6, L12, L16, L22, L23, M1, M6, M7, M8, M11, M13, M17, N1, N2, N3, N7, N8, N9, N11, N16, N17, N23, O1, O7, O8, O9, P1, P7, P9, P10, P11, Q1, Q6, Q11, Q13, Q15, Q16, R1, R6, R10, R11, S3, S11, S15, S17, S18, S20, S23, T1, T2, T5, T7, T14, T17, U1, U4, V9, V11, W1, W4, X1, X7, X8, Y1, Y5, Y8, Y9, Y11, Z3, Z6, Z12, Z16, Z20
Jōyō Kanji (284)
LE7, LE9, LE14 - LE24, RI8, TO7, TO12, BO3, BO5, FR6, FR7, A1 - A17, A20 - A22, B1 - B7, B12, B13, C1, C4 - C8, C10, C12 - C20, D1, D2, D4, D6, D8 - D14, E1 - E5, E7, E9 - E13, F1 - F5, F7, F9 - F11, G1 - G3, G7 - G10, G12, G13, H1 - H8, H11, I1 - I4, I6 - I12, I15 - I18, J1, J4 - J8, J10 - J12, K5 - K7, K9, K11, K12, L4, L5, L7, L8, L9, L11, L14, L15, L16, L18, L19, L20, L22, L24, M3 - M9, M11, M13, M14, M15, M17, N2, N3, N4, N6, N10 - N15, N17, N18, N20, N22, O1 - O5, O8 - O10, P1, P2, P3, P7, P9 - P11, P13, P14, Q2, Q3, Q4, Q6, Q7, Q9, Q10, Q11, Q15, Q16, Q17, R1 - R5, R8 - R11, S2, S4, S5, S6, S9, S12, S15, S16, S17, S19, S21, S22, S26, T3 - T10, T14, T15, T17, U3 - U6, V1, V2, V3, V6 - V9, V11, V13, V15, V18, W3, W7, W8, W11, X9, X10, X11, Y2 - Y5, Y8 - Y12, Y15, Y16, Y17, Z3, Z4, Z9, Z12, Z13, Z16, Z21
Other kanji (66)
TO1, A18, B8, B9, B11, B14, B15, C2, C3, D3, D5, E8, F12, G6, H10, I5, I19, J3, J9, K1, K4, K8, L10, L13, L17, L21, M10, M12, N5, N21, N24, N25, P6, P12, P16, Q5, Q12, Q14, R7, S1, S7, S8, S10, S14, T12, T13, T16, U2, V5, V10, V17, W5, W9, W10, W12, X2, X4, Y7, Y13, Y14, Z7, Z8, Z11, Z14, Z15, Z19
Graphemes defined by the authors (57)
TO3, TO4, TO9, TO11, BO1, FR2, B10, C11, D7, F6, F8, H9, I13, I14, J2, K2, K10, L2, L3, M2, M16, M18, M19, M20, N19, O6, P4, P5, P8, P15, Q8, S13, S24, S25, T11, T18, V4, V12, V14, V16, V19, V20, V21, V22, W2, W6, X3, X5, X6, Y6, Z1, Z2, Z5, Z10, Z17, Z18, Z22

Table 1: Origin of the graphemes

あ a	か ka	さ sa	た ta	な na	は ha	ま ma	や ya	ら ra	わ wa	ん n
い i	き ki	し shi	ち chi	に ni	ひ hi	み mi		り ri		
う u	く ku	す su	つ tsu	ぬ nu	ふ fu	む mu	ゆ yu	る ru		
え e	け ke	せ se	て te	ね ne	へ he	め me		れ re		
お o	こ ko	そ so	と to	の no	ほ ho	も mo	よ yo	ろ ro	を wo	

Table 2: Hiragana Chart

ア a	カ ka	サ sa	タ ta	ナ na	ハ ha	マ ma	ヤ ya	ラ ra	ワ wa	ン n
イ i	キ ki	シ shi	チ chi	ニ ni	ヒ hi	ミ mi		リ ri		
ウ u	ク ku	ス su	ツ tsu	ヌ nu	フ fu	ム mu	ユ yu	ル ru		
エ e	ケ ke	セ se	テ te	ネ ne	ヘ he	メ me		レ re		
オ o	コ ko	ソ so	ト to	ノ no	ホ ho	モ mo	ヨ yo	ロ ro	ヲ wo	

Table 3: Katakana Chart

THE GRAPHEMES

	LE	RI	TO	BO	EN	FR	A	B	C	D	E	F	G	H	I	J
								口	日	田	丁	十	𠂆	⺧	土	木
1	冫	彡	䒑	八	厂	丶	一	口	日	田	丁	十	千	牛	土	木
2	氵	刂	⺌	儿	广	㐅	二	言	旦	苗	了	斗	舌	告	吉	采
3	忄	阝	マ	心	疒	丨	人	占	亘	畾	矛	古	重	先	士	桑
4	丬	卩	⺈	灬	辶	卜	山	加	旧	魚	可	固	禾	生	赤	林
5	亻	攵	宀	月	廴	巾	石	召	白	曽	奇	早	乖	朱	圭	麻
6	禾	頁	艹		囗	土	耳	豆	原	由	牙	𠦝	壬	失	孝	本
7	米	隹	⺮			大	火	兄	百	甶	示	干	廷	矢	者	未
8	阝	月	罒				川	兑	門	曲	于	缶	手	午	工	末
9	弓		⺍				力	𠂤	艮	曹	才	平	乗	隺	五	朮
10	犭		爫				刀	吕	良	甲	寸	羊	垂	乍	並	米
11	扌		𠂉				女	呂	鳥	申	付	半	彳	竹	亜	東
12	礻		⻗				小	中	車	里	寺	丰	行		西	東
13	衤						少	虫	目	単	専	韋	升		龶	
14	糸						皿	虫	相	果			隹		堇	
15	王						子	串	且						青	
16	木						母		自						責	
17	言						父		首						王	
18	足						乂		見						主	
19	酉						凵		貝						⺷	
20	食						斤		則							
21	金						丘									
22	馬						羽									
23	日															
24	月															
25																
26																

	K	L	M	N	O	P	Q	R	S	T	U	V	W	X	Y	Z
	廿	冖	亠	乚	止	以	厶	又	勹	𠆢	尸	𠂇	弋	ヨ	匚	
1	冉	冖	亠	乚	止	水	厶	又	奂	癶	尸	右	弋	ヨ	匚	乚
2	开	𭕄	㐭	乙	歩	永	台	取	免	𠆢	辟	有	弐	翟	区	𠂤
3	廾	尚	京	心	延	求	能	叔	勹	介	尺	布	代	尋	匹	非
4	廿	売	市	必	卸	氺	広	隻	勺	余	戸	𠂇	戈	帚	巨	不
5	革	軍	亡	宂	正	氼	云	祭	句	金	扁	𠂇	戋	录	臣	無
6	甘	冂	方	元	疋	襄	至	殳	旬	舎	倉	友	戠	彐	臣	片
7	某	内	文	酉	疋	衣	去	圣	曷	食		史	我	隶	臤	厂
8	其	同	斉	尢	足	䒑	亠	奴	勿	令		更	義	聿	馬	乃
9	井	周	交	匕	走	長	育	反	万	今		大	戊	兼	己	及
10	卄	冎	亦	化	是	辰	充	支	昜	合		莫	戌	君	包	丁
11	昔	罔	立	比		氏	鬼	皮	豕	㑒		犬	成	争	弓	之
12	共	而	音	北		氐	亥		家	俞		尞	戔		弔	為
13		禺	音	旨		民	幺		彖	侖		天			弗	入
14		月	章	兆		以	丝		貇	八		关			丂	並
15		肖	意	七		卯	玄		欠	公		夫			考	敢
16		用	亲	乇		卬	糸		次	谷		莫			与	身
17		甫	辛	毛			系		夕	谷		夬			呉	产
18		円	产	屯					舛	六		央				丿
19		冊	冋	电					名			夹				敝
20		再	产	九					歹			关				鬲
21		冓		夲					列			𡗗				世
22		舟		丸					久			丰				亜
23		几		巳					夂							
24		凡		巴					复							
25				也					夋							
26									各